Egyptian Mythology

A Comprehensive Guide to Egyptian Mythology including Myths, Art, Religion, and Culture

TABLE OF CONTENTS

INTRODUCTION 6
PREFACE 9
PART 1 11
  CHAPTER 1 11
    THE ORIGIN OF THE MYTH 11
  CHAPTER 2 21
    SOURCES 21
  CHAPTER 3 43
    COSMOLOGY 43
PART 2 – MAJOR MYTHS 45
  CHAPTER 4 45
    MYTHS 45
    CREATION 47
    ANCIENT EGYPTIAN CREATION MYTHS 50
    THE REIGN OF THE SUN GOD "RA" 52
  CHAPTER 5 54
    OSIRIS MYTH 54
  CHAPTER 6 59
    THE JOURNEY OF THE SUN GOD 59
    END OF THE UNIVERSE 69
PART 3 78
  CHAPTER 7 78
    INFLUENCE IN EGYPTIAN CULTURE 78
  CHAPTER 8 82

INFLUENCE OF MYTHOLOGY IN EGYPTIAN RELIGILION 82
INFLUENCE OF MYTHOLOGY IN EGYPTIAN ART 85
INFLUENCE OF MYTHOLOGY IN EGYPTIAN LITERATURE 90
CHAPTER 9 91
ENDING CHAPTER ABOUT HER - IMPORTANT PART OF ANCIENT EGYPT 91
CHAPTER 10 95
CONCLUSION 95
DISCLAIMER 99

Copyright 2020 by Historical Publishing - All rights reserved.

This document is geared towards providing exact and reliable information in regards to the topic and issue covered. The publication is sold with the idea that the publisher is not required to render accounting, officially permitted, or otherwise, qualified services. If advice is necessary, legal or professional, a practiced individual in the profession should be ordered.

- From a Declaration of Principles which was accepted and approved equally by a Committee of the American Bar Association and a Committee of Publishers and Associations.

In no way is it legal to reproduce, duplicate, or transmit any part of this document in either electronic means or in printed format. Recording of this publication is strictly prohibited and any storage of this document is not allowed unless with written permission from the publisher. All rights reserved.

The information provided herein is stated to be truthful and consistent, in that any liability, in terms of inattention or otherwise, by any usage or abuse of any policies, processes, or directions contained within is the solitary and utter responsibility of the recipient reader. Under no circumstances will any legal responsibility or blame be held against the publisher for any reparation, damages, or monetary loss due to the information herein, either directly or indirectly.

Respective authors own all copyrights not held by the publisher.

The information herein is offered for informational purposes solely, and is universal as so. The presentation of the information is without contract or any type of guarantee assurance.

The trademarks that are used are without any consent, and the publication of the trademark is without permission or backing by the trademark owner. All trademarks and brands within this book are for clarifying purposes only and are the owned by the owners themselves, not affiliated with this document.

INTRODUCTION

Egyptian Mythology is the accumulation of myths derived from ancient Egypt from at least c. 4000 BCE to 30 CE. The end was marked with the death Cleopatra VII, the last of the Ptolemaic sovereign of Egypt.

Often in Egyptian writing and art, myths occur— particularly in short stories and in religious materials such as ritual texts, hymns, funerary texts and temple decorations. Full accounts of the myth from these sources are rare as they are habitually described in brief fragments.

The Egyptian religion and belief were spread beyond the domain of Egypt through trade, notably after 130 BCE when the Silk Road opened. This made Alexandria the epicenter of commerce. For other cultures, the imperative aspect of Egyptian Mythology was the eternal life after death concept, the reincarnation and benevolent deities. Both Greek philosophers Plato and Pythagoras are believed to be inspired by the belief of Egyptians in reincarnation. What's more, religious cultures from Egypt were largely adopted by the Romans as they did from other civilization.

Natural surroundings greatly influenced the Egyptian myth. Annually, the Nile flooded the land to renew the soil's richness and promote the prosperity of farming that was essential to the civilization of Egypt. Daily, the sun rose and set to bless the land with light and to watch over the activities of humanity. Thus, in the view of Egyptians, water and the sun were considered the emblems of life. They also viewed time as a chain of natural cycles. Low and high floods threatened the order of this cycle; they caused damage to the cultivation and buildings and brought about famine. The generous Nile valley was encircled by a severe desert that was inhabited by peoples who the Egyptians believed were savage foes who disrupted the order. As a result, they believed their area of habitation was one of stability, secluded from the rest.

To the Egyptians, humanity's existence was believed to be only a tiny part in the journey to eternity. The deities and supernatural agents coordinated and ruled over the course of this voyage.

According to the historian Bunsen:
"Heh, called Huh in some eras, was one of the original gods of the Ogdoad [the eight deities worshipped during the Old Kingdom, 2575-2134 BCE] at Hermopolis and represented eternity – the goal and destiny of all human life in Egyptian religious beliefs, a stage of existence in which mortals could attain everlasting bliss (86)."

The existence of someone on this earth was a part of the eternal journey; it was also an introduction to something bigger. The concept of the afterlife for Egyptians was a mirror-world of one's life on earth— particularly, one's life in Egypt. If one desired to enjoy the rest of his/her eternal journey, he was obliged to live that life correctly.

The Creation of the World
The creation of the universe and the world out of whirling chaos and obscurity was where the journey commenced. There was once nothing but infinite dark water, devoid of form or purpose. From this bedlam surfaced Ben-Ben (the primeval hill); atop of this hill lived Atum (sometimes, Ptah). Atum observed the emptiness and realized his loneliness. He bred with his shadow to produce two offspring: Tefnut (goddess of moisture, whom Atum vomited out) and Shu (god of air, whom Atum spat out). The principles of order were issued by Tefnut and the principles of life were given by Shu.

After they were born, the siblings set out to create the world, leaving their father on the Ben-Ben. After a while, Atum was overwhelmed by anxiety as his children took a long time to return. He took out his one eye and sent it to look for them. Much to his relief, Shu and Tefnut returned after some time with his one eye; Atum, grateful for his children's return, shed tears of happiness. His tears rained atop the dark and fertile soil of Ben-Ben, thereby producing women and men.

These early beings had no place to dwell, however. Tefnut and Shu, thus, mated and bore the goddess Nut (the Sky) and the god Geb (the earth). The siblings, Geb and Nut, became lovers, inseparable from one another. Unable to accept their unacceptable behavior, Atum took Nut into the heavens, far away from Geb. Both lovers had clear views of one another; however, they were unable to touch. Already impregnated by Geb, Nut gave birth to Set, Osiris, Isis and Nephthys— the prominent Egyptian gods. Osiris was often considered a sensible and thoughtful god which was probably why Atum gave him rule over the world.

PREFACE

This book "Egyptian Mythology" is intended for students, and is based on the various gods of ancient Egypt who formed the religion of the era and helped explain the world and the reasons many things occur. Most of the Egyptian Mythology is taken from the religious writings, arts, short stories, temple decorations as well as other texts discovered over the years. Most of the myths and stories recovered were incomplete or in fragments.

The book is intended entirely for the general public, who are increasingly interested in the religion and civilisation of ancient Egypt, but whose only means of obtaining knowledge of that country is apparently through magazine stories in which a mummy is the principal character. It may be worth noting that in these legends of ancient Egypt mummies are not mentioned, except in the Duat, the home of the dead, where one naturally expects to find them.

Though the book is intended for the unscientific reader, I have made some provision for the more serious student, in the Notes at the end. In these I have given the origin of the legend, the book or books in which that original is published, and the book where the translation into a modern language by one of the great scholars of the day can be found. Other translations there are in plenty, which can be seen in specialist libraries; many of these, however, are of use only to a student of Egyptian literature and language.

In this book, I have retold the legends of the Gods of ancient Egypt, legends, which were current in the "morning of the world," preserved to the present day engraved on stone and written on papyri.

A prolonged study of the religious and mythological texts of ancient Egypt has convinced me of the futility of attempting to reconcile the conflicting beliefs and to harmonize the contradictory statements which are found in them, so long as we regard the Egyptian religion as " one in its extension and principle." It must first of all be resolved into its constituent elements, and when this has been done, it will probably be possible to classify, and arrange, and assign to their proper sources the various material and spiritual conceptions and beliefs which the Egyptians heaped up in their minds and flung together in their religious writings. It must, moreover, be studied by the light which the science of
comparative religion has given us, and due regard must be paid to the important evidence on the subject that may be deduced from the remains and monuments of the Predynastic and Archaic Periods which have been unearthed during the last few years.

PART 1
CHAPTER 1

THE ORIGIN OF THE MYTH

The development of Egyptian myths are a series of ancient accounts concerning the origins of the sun, earth, moon and stars as well as the creation of life. While there are many variations on the myth, the one originating at Heliopolis -- one of the oldest cities along the Nile -- is perhaps the most well-known. The story tells of several deities and the role each played in creation. Ra, the god of the sun, is the primary deity in the myth, but other gods, including Khnum and Nut, play a part. The Egyptian creation myth takes place over a period of seven days, similar to the Hebrew creation story.
For almost 30 centuries—from its unification around 3100 B.C. to its conquest by Alexander the Great in 332 B.C.—ancient Egypt was the preeminent civilization in the Mediterranean world. From the great pyramids of the Old Kingdom through the military conquests of the New Kingdom, Egypt's majesty has long entranced archaeologists and historians and created a vibrant field of study all its own: Egyptology. The main sources of information about ancient Egypt are the many monuments, objects and artifacts that have been recovered from archaeological sites, covered with hieroglyphs that have only recently been deciphered. The picture that emerges is of a culture with few equals in the beauty of its art, the accomplishment of its architecture or the richness of its religious traditions.

Predynastic Period (c. 5000-3100 B.C.)
Few written records or artifacts have been found from the Predynastic Period, which encompassed at least 2,000 years of gradual development of the Egyptian civilization.
Neolithic (late Stone Age) communities in northeastern Africa exchanged hunting for agriculture and made early advances that paved the way for the later development of Egyptian arts and crafts, technology, politics and religion (including a great reverence for the dead and possibly a belief in life after death). Around 3400 B.C., two separate kingdoms were established: the Red Land to the north, based in the Nile River Delta and extending along the Nile perhaps to Atfih; and the White Land in the south, stretching from Atfih to Gebel es-Silsila. A southern king, Scorpion, made the first attempts to conquer the northern kingdom around 3200 B.C. A century later, King Menes would subdue the north and unify the country, becoming the first king of the first dynasty.

Archaic (Early Dynastic) Period (c. 3100-2686 B.C.)
King Menes founded the capital of ancient Egypt at White Walls (later known as Memphis), in the north, near the apex of the Nile River delta. The capital would grow into a great metropolis that dominated Egyptian society during the Old Kingdom period. The Archaic Period saw the development of the foundations of Egyptian society, including the all-important ideology of kingship. To the ancient Egyptians, the king was a godlike being, closely identified with the all-powerful god Horus. The earliest known hieroglyphic writing also dates to this period.
In the Archaic Period, as in all other periods, most ancient Egyptians were farmers living in small villages, and agriculture (largely wheat and barley) formed the economic

base of the Egyptian state. The annual flooding of the great Nile River provided the necessary irrigation and fertilization each year; farmers sowed the wheat after the flooding receded and harvested it before the season of high temperatures and drought returned.

Old Kingdom: Age of the Pyramid Builders (c. 2686-2181 B.C.)

The Old Kingdom began with the third dynasty of pharaohs. Around 2630 B.C., the third dynasty's King Djoser asked Imhotep, an architect, priest and healer, to design a funerary monument for him; the result was the world's first major stone building, the Step-Pyramid at Saqqara, near Memphis. Pyramid-building reached its zenith with the construction of the Great Pyramid at Giza, on the outskirts of Cairo. Built for Khufu (or Cheops, in Greek), who ruled from 2589 to 2566 B.C., the pyramid was later named by classical historians as one of the ancient world's Seven Wonders. Two other pyramids were built at Giza for Khufu's successors Khafra (2558-2532 B.C) and Menkaura (2532-2503 B.C.).

During the third and fourth dynasties, Egypt enjoyed a golden age of peace and prosperity. The pharaohs held absolute power and provided a stable central government; the kingdom faced no serious threats from abroad; and successful military campaigns in foreign countries like Nubia and Libya added to its considerable economic prosperity. Over the course of the fifth and sixth dynasties, the king's wealth was steadily depleted, partially due to the huge expense of pyramid-building, and his absolute power faltered in the face of the growing influence of the nobility and the priesthood that grew up around the sun god Ra (Re). After the death of the sixth dynasty's King Pepy II, who ruled for some 94 years, the Old Kingdom period ended in chaos.

First Intermediate Period (c. 2181-2055 B.C.)
On the heels of the Old Kingdom's collapse, the seventh and eighth dynasties consisted of a rapid succession of Memphis-based rulers until about 2160 B.C., when the central authority completely dissolved, leading to civil war between provincial governors. This chaotic situation was intensified by Bedouin invasions and accompanied by famine and disease.

From this era of conflict emerged two different kingdoms: A line of 17 rulers (dynasties nine and 10) based in Heracleopolis ruled Middle Egypt between Memphis and Thebes, while another family of rulers arose in Thebes to challenge Heracleopolitan power. Around 2055 B.C., the Theban prince Mentuhotep managed to topple Heracleopolis and reunited Egypt, beginning the 11th dynasty and ending the First Intermediate Period.

Middle Kingdom: 12th Dynasty (c. 2055-1786 B.C.)
After the last ruler of the 11th dynasty, Mentuhotep IV, was assassinated, the throne passed to his vizier, or chief minister, who became King Amenemhet I, founder of dynasty 12. A new capital was established at It-towy, south of Memphis, while Thebes remained a great religious center. During the Middle Kingdom, Egypt once again flourished, as it had during the Old Kingdom. The 12th dynasty kings ensured the smooth succession of their line by making each successor co-regent, a custom that began with Amenemhet I.

Middle-Kingdom Egypt pursued an aggressive foreign policy, colonizing Nubia (with its rich supply of gold, ebony, ivory and other resources) and repelling the Bedouins who had infiltrated Egypt during the First Intermediate Period. The kingdom also built diplomatic and trade relations with Syria, Palestine and other countries; undertook building projects including military fortresses and mining quarries; and returned to pyramid-building in the tradition of the Old Kingdom. The Middle Kingdom reached its peak under Amenemhet III (1842-1797 B.C.); its decline began under Amenenhet IV (1798-1790 B.C.) and continued under his sister and regent, Queen Sobekneferu (1789-1786 B.C.), who was the first confirmed female ruler of Egypt and the last ruler of the 12th dynasty.

Second Intermediate Period (c. 1786-1567 B.C.)
The 13th dynasty marked the beginning of another unsettled period in Egyptian history, during which a rapid succession of kings failed to consolidate power. As a consequence, during the Second Intermediate Period Egypt was divided into several spheres of influence. The official royal court and seat of government was relocated to Thebes, while a rival dynasty (the 14th), centered on the city of Xois in the Nile delta, seems to have existed at the same time as the 13th.
Around 1650 B.C., a line of foreign rulers known as the Hyksos took advantage of Egypt's instability to take control. The Hyksos rulers of the 15th dynasty adopted and continued many of the existing Egyptian traditions in government as well as culture. They ruled concurrently with the line of native Theban rulers of the 17th dynasty, who retained control over most of southern Egypt despite having to pay taxes to the Hyksos. (The 16th dynasty is variously believed to be Theban or Hyksos rulers.) Conflict eventually flared between the two groups, and the Thebans launched a war against the Hyksos around 1570 B.C., driving them out of Egypt.

New Kingdom (c. 1567-1085 B.C.)
Under Ahmose I, the first king of the 18th dynasty, Egypt was once again reunited. During the 18th dynasty, Egypt restored its control over Nubia and began military campaigns in

Palestine, clashing with other powers in the area such as the Mitannians and the Hittites. The country went on to establish the world's first great empire, stretching from Nubia to the Euphrates River in Asia. In addition to powerful kings such as Amenhotep I (1546-1526 B.C.), Thutmose I (1525-1512 B.C.) and Amenhotep III (1417-1379 B.C.), the New Kingdom was notable for the role of royal women such as Queen Hatshepsut (1503-1482 B.C.), who began ruling as a regent for her young stepson (he later became Thutmose III, Egypt's greatest military hero), but rose to wield all the powers of a pharaoh.

The controversial Amenhotep IV (c. 1379-1362), of the late 18th dynasty, undertook a religious revolution, disbanding the priesthoods dedicated to Amon-Re (a combination of the local Theban god Amon and the sun god Re) and forcing the exclusive worship of another sun-god, Aton. Renaming himself Akhenaton ("servant of the Aton"), he built a new capital in Middle Egypt called Akhetaton, known later as Amarna. Upon Akhenaton's death, the capital returned to Thebes and Egyptians returned to worshiping a multitude of gods. The 19th and 20th dynasties, known as the Ramesside period (for the line of kings named Ramses) saw the restoration of the weakened Egyptian empire and an impressive amount of building, including great temples and cities. According to biblical chronology, the Exodus of Moses and the Israelites from Egypt possibly occurred during the reign of Ramses II (1304-1237 B.C.).

All of the New Kingdom rulers (with the exception of Akhenaton) were laid to rest in deep, rock-cut tombs (not pyramids) in the Valley of the Kings, a burial site on the west bank of the Nile opposite Thebes. Most of them were raided and destroyed, with the exception of the tomb and treasure of Tutankhamen (c.1361-1352 B.C.), discovered largely intact in A.D. 1922. The splendid mortuary temple of the last great king of the 20th dynasty, Ramses III (c. 1187-1156 B.C.), was also relatively well preserved, and indicated the prosperity Egypt still enjoyed during his reign. The kings who followed Ramses III were less successful: Egypt lost its provinces in Palestine and Syria for good and suffered from foreign invasions (notably by the Libyans), while its wealth was being steadily but inevitably depleted.

Third Intermediate Period (c. 1085-664 B.C.)
The next 400 years–known as the Third Intermediate Period– saw important changes in Egyptian politics, society and culture. Centralized government under the 21st dynasty pharaohs gave way to the resurgence of local officials, while foreigners from Libya and Nubia grabbed power for themselves and left a lasting imprint on Egypt's population. The 22nd dynasty began around 945 B.C. with King Sheshonq, a descendant of Libyans who had invaded Egypt during the late 20th dynasty and settled there. Many local rulers were virtually autonomous during this period and dynasties 23-24 are poorly documented.

In the eighth century B.C., Nubian pharaohs beginning with Shabako, ruler of the Nubian kingdom of Kush, established their own dynasty–the 25th–at Thebes. Under Kushite rule, Egypt clashed with the growing Assyrian empire. In 671 B.C., the Assyrian ruler Esarhaddon drove the Kushite king Taharka out of Memphis and destroyed the city; he then appointed his own rulers out of local governors and officials loyal to the Assyrians. One of them, Necho of Sais, ruled briefly as the first king of the 26th dynasty before being killed by the Kushite leader Tanuatamun, in a final, unsuccessful grab for power.

From the Late Period to Alexander's Conquest (c.664-332 B.C.)

Beginning with Necho's son, Psammetichus, the Saite dynasty ruled a reunified Egypt for less than two centuries. In 525 B.C., Cambyses, king of Persia, defeated Psammetichus III, the last Saite king, at the Battle of Pelusium, and Egypt became part of the Persian Empire. Persian rulers such as Darius (522-485 B.C.) ruled the country largely under the same terms as native Egyptian kings: Darius supported Egypt's religious cults and undertook the building and restoration of its temples. The tyrannical rule of Xerxes (486-465 B.C.) sparked increased uprisings under him and his successors. One of these rebellions triumphed in 404 B.C., beginning one last period of Egyptian independence under native rulers (dynasties 28-30). In the mid-fourth century B.C., the Persians again attacked Egypt, reviving their empire under Ataxerxes III in 343 B.C. Barely a decade later, in 332 B.C., Alexander the Great of Macedonia defeated the armies of the Persian Empire and conquered Egypt. After Alexander's death, Egypt was ruled by a line of Macedonian kings, beginning with Alexander's general Ptolemy and continuing with his descendants. The last ruler of Ptolemaic Egypt–the legendary Cleopatra VII–surrendered Egypt to the armies of Octavian (later Augustus) in 31 B.C. Six centuries of Roman rule followed, during which Christianity became the official religion of Rome and its provinces (including Egypt). The conquest of Egypt by the Arabs in the seventh century A.D. and the introduction of Islam would do away with the last outward aspects of ancient Egyptian culture and propel the country towards its modern incarnation.

DIVINE ORIGIN OF KINGS

Egyptians were a nation of men who were wholly given up to the worship of beasts and the cult of the dead.

The Egyptians, however, acted in a perfectly logical manner, for they believed that they were a divine nation, and that they were ruled by kings who were themselves gods incarnate; their earliest kings, they asserted, were actually gods, who did not disdain to live upon earth, and to go about and up and down through it, and to mingle with men. Other ancient nations were content to believe that they had been brought into being by the power of their gods operating upon matter, but the Egyptians believed that they were the issue of the great God who created the universe, and that they were of directly divine origin. When the gods ceased to reign in their proper persons upon earth, they were succeeded by a series of demi-gods, who were in turn succeeded by the Manes, and these were duly followed by kings in whom was enshrined a divine nature with characteristic attributes. When the physical or natural body of a king died, the divine portion of his being, i.e., the spiritual body, returned to its original abode with the gods, and it was duly worshipped by men upon earth as a god and with the gods. This happy result was partly brought about by the performance of certain ceremonies, which were at first wholly magical, but later partly magical and partly religious, and by the recital of appropriate words uttered in the duly prescribed tone and manner, and by the keeping of festivals at the tombs at stated seasons when the appointed offerings were made, and the prayers for the welfare of the dead were said. From the earliest times the worship of the gods went hand in hand with the deification of dead kings and other royal personages, and the worship of departed monarchs from some aspects may be regarded as meritorious as the worship of the gods. From one point of view Egypt was as much a land of gods as of men, and the inhabitants of the country wherein the gods lived and moved naturally devoted a considerable portion of their time upon earth to the worship of divine beings and of their ancestors who had departed to the land of the gods. In the matter of religion, and all that appertains thereto, the Egyptians were a "peculiar people," and in all ages they have exhibited a tenacity of belief and a conservatism which distinguish them from all the other great nations of antiquity.

CHAPTER 2

SOURCES

Religion sources

Ancient Egyptian religion was a complex system of polytheistic beliefs and rituals which were an integral part of ancient Egyptian society. It centered on the Egyptians' interaction with a multitude of deities who were believed to be present in, and in control of, the forces and elements of nature. The myths about these gods were meant to explain the origins and behavior of the forces they represented. The practices of Egyptian religion were efforts to provide for the gods and gain their favor.

Formal religious practice centered on the pharaoh, the king of Egypt. Although he was a human, the pharaoh was believed to be descended from the gods. He acted as the intermediary between his people and the gods, and was obligated to sustain the gods through rituals and offerings so that they could maintain order in the universe. Therefore, the state dedicated enormous resources to the performance of these rituals and to the construction of the temples where they were carried out. Individuals could also interact with the gods for their own purposes, appealing for their help through prayer or compelling them to act through magic. These popular religious practices were distinct from, but closely linked with, the formal rituals and institutions. The popular religious tradition grew more prominent in the course of Egyptian history as the status of the pharaoh declined. Another important aspect of the religion was the belief in the afterlife and funerary practices.

The Egyptians made great efforts to ensure the survival of their souls after death, providing tombs, grave goods, and offerings to preserve the bodies and spirits of the deceased.

The religion had its roots in Egypt's prehistory and lasted for more than 3,000 years. The details of religious belief changed over time as the importance of particular gods rose and declined, and their intricate relationships shifted. At various times certain gods became preeminent over the others, including the sun god Ra, the creator god Amun, and the mother goddess Isis. For a brief period, in the aberrant theology promulgated by the pharaoh Akhenaten, a single god, the Aten, replaced the traditional pantheon. Yet the overall system endured, even through several periods of foreign rule, until the coming of Christianity in the early centuries AD. It left behind numerous religious writings and monuments, along with significant influences on cultures both ancient and modern.

Egyptian religion was a combination of beliefs and practices which, in the modern day, would include magic, mythology, science, medicine, psychiatry, spiritualism, herbology, as well as the modern understanding of 'religion' as belief in a higher power and a life after death. Religion played a part in every aspect of the lives of the ancient Egyptians because life on earth was seen as only one part of an eternal journey, and in order to continue that journey after death, one needed to live a life worthy of continuance.

During one's life on earth, one was expected to uphold the principle of ma'at (harmony) with an understanding that one's actions in life affected not only one's self but others' lives as well, and the operation of the universe. People were expected to depend on each other to keep balance as this was the will of the gods to produce the greatest amount of pleasure and happiness for humans through a harmonious existence which also enabled the gods to better perform their tasks.

By honoring the principle of ma'at (personified as a goddess of the same name holding the white feather of truth) and living one's life in accordance with its precepts, one was aligned with the gods and the forces of light against the forces of darkness and chaos, and assured one's self of a welcome reception in the Hall of Truth after death and a gentle judgment by Osiris, the Lord of the Dead.

The Gods

The underlying principle of Egyptian religion was known as heka (magic) personified in the god Heka. Heka had always existed and was present in the act of creation. He was the god of magic and medicine but was also the power which enabled the gods to perform their functions and allowed human beings to commune with their gods. He was all-pervasive and all-encompassing, imbuing the daily lives of the Egyptians with magic and meaning and sustaining the principle of ma'at upon which life depended.

Possibly the best way to understand Heka is in terms of money: one is able to purchase a particular item with a certain denomination of currency because that item's value is considered the same, or less, than that denomination. The bill in one's hand has an invisible value given it by a standard of worth (once upon a time the gold standard) which promises a merchant it will compensate for what one is buying. This is exactly the relationship of Heka to the gods and human existence: he was the standard, the foundation of power, on which everything else depended. A god or goddess was invoked for a specific purpose, was worshipped for what they had given, but it was Heka who enabled this relationship between the people and their deities.

The gods of ancient Egypt were seen as the lords of creation and custodians of order but also as familiar friends who were interested in helping and guiding the people of the land. The gods had created order out of chaos and given the people the most beautiful land on earth. Egyptians were so deeply attached to their homeland that they shunned prolonged military campaigns beyond their borders for fear they would die on foreign soil and would not be given the proper rites for their continued journey after life. Egyptian monarchs refused to give their daughters in marriage to foreign rulers for the same reason. The gods of Egypt had blessed the land with their special favor, and the people were expected to honor them as great and kindly benefactors.

"THE GODS OF ANCIENT EGYPT WERE SEEN AS THE LORDS OF CREATION AND CUSTODIANS OF ORDER BUT ALSO AS FAMILIAR FRIENDS WHO WERE INTERESTED IN HELPING AND GUIDING THE PEOPLE OF THE LAND."

Long ago, they believed, there had been nothing but the dark swirling waters of chaos stretching into eternity. Out of this chaos (Nu) rose the primordial hill, known as the Ben-Ben, upon which stood the great god Atum (some versions say the god was Ptah) in the presence of Heka. Atum looked upon the nothingness and recognized his aloneness, and so he mated with his own shadow to give birth to two children, Shu (god of air, whom Atum spat out) and Tefnut (goddess of moisture, whom Atum vomited out). Shu gave to the early world the principles of life while Tefnut contributed the principles of order. Leaving their father on the Ben-Ben, they set out to establish the world.

In time, Atum became concerned because his children were gone so long, and so he removed his eye and sent it in search of them. While his eye was gone, Atum sat alone on the hill in the midst of chaos and contemplated eternity. Shu and Tefnut returned with the eye of Atum (later associated with the Udjat eye, the Eye of Ra, or the All-Seeing Eye) and their father, grateful for their safe return, shed tears of joy. These tears, dropping onto the dark, fertile earth of the Ben-Ben, gave birth to men and women.

These humans had nowhere to live, however, and so Shu and Tefnut mated and gave birth to Geb (the earth) and Nut (the sky). Geb and Nut, though brother and sister, fell deeply in love and were inseparable. Atum found their behaviour unacceptable and pushed Nut away from Geb, high up into the heavens. The two lovers were forever able to see each other but were no longer able to touch. Nut was already pregnant by Geb, however, and eventually gave birth to Osiris, Isis, Set, Nephthys, and Horus – the five Egyptian gods most often recognized as the earliest (although Hathor is now considered to be older than Isis). These gods then gave birth to all the other gods in one form or another.

Horus Statuette

The gods each had their own area of speciality. Bastet, for example, was the goddess of the hearth, homelife, women's health and secrets, and of cats. Hathor was the goddess of kindness and love, associated with gratitude and generosity, motherhood, and compassion. According to one early story surrounding her, however, she was originally the goddess Sekhmet who became drunk on blood and almost destroyed the world until she was pacified and put to sleep by beer which the gods had dyed red to fool her. When she awoke from her sleep, she was transformed into a gentler deity. Although she was associated with beer, Tenenet was the principle goddess of beer and also presided over childbirth. Beer was considered essential for one's health in ancient Egypt and a gift from the gods, and there were many deities associated with the drink which was said to have been first brewed by Osiris.

An early myth tells of how Osiris was tricked and killed by his brother Set and how Isis brought him back to life. He was incomplete, however, as a fish had eaten a part of him, and so he could no longer rule harmoniously on earth and was made Lord of the Dead in the underworld. His son, Horus the Younger, battled Set for eighty years and finally defeated him to restore harmony to the land. Horus and Isis then ruled together, and all the other gods found their places and areas of expertise to help and encourage the people of Egypt.

Among the most important of these gods were the three who made up the Theban Triad: Amun, Mut, and Knons (also known as Khonsu). Amun was a local fertility god of Thebes until the Theban noble Menuhotep II (2061-2010 BCE) defeated his rivals and united Egypt, elevating Thebes to the position of capital and its gods to supremacy. Amun, Mut, and Khons of Upper Egypt (where Thebes was located) took on the attributes of Ptah, Sekhment, and Khonsu of Lower Egypt who were much older deities. Amun became the supreme creator god, symbolized by the sun; Mut was his wife, symbolized by the sun's rays and the all-seeing eye; and Khons was their son, the god of healing and destroyer of evil spirits.

These three gods were associated with Ogdoad of Hermopolis, a group of eight primordial deities who "embodied the qualities of primeval matter, such as darkness, moistness, and lack of boundaries or visible powers. It usually consisted of four deities doubled to eight by including female counterparts" (Pinch, 175-176). The Ogdoad (pronounced OG-doh-ahd) represented the state of the cosmos before land rose from the waters of chaos and light broke through the primordial darkness and were also referred to as the Hehu (`the infinities'). They were Amun and Amaunet, Heh and Hauhet, Kek and Kauket, and Nun and Naunet each representing a different aspect of the formless and unknowable time before creation: Hiddenness (Amun/Amaunet), Infinity (Heh/Hauhet), Darkness (Kek/Kauket), and the Abyss (Nut/Naunet). The Ogdoad are the best example of the Egyptian's insistence on symmetry and balance in all things embodied in their male/female aspect which was thought to have engendered the principle of harmony in the cosmos before the birth of the world.

Harmony & Eternity

The Egyptians believed that the earth (specifically Egypt) reflected the cosmos. The stars in the night sky and the constellations they formed were thought to have a direct bearing on one's personality and future fortunes. The gods informed the night sky, even traveled through it, but were not distant deities in the heavens; the gods lived alongside the people of Egypt and interacted with them daily. Trees were considered the homes of the gods and one of the most popular of the Egyptian deities, Hathor, was sometimes known as "Mistress of the Date Palm" or "The Lady of the Sycamore" because she was thought to favor these particular trees to rest in or beneath. Scholars Oakes and Gahlin note that

"Presumably because of the shade and the fruit provided by them, goddesses associated with protection, mothering, and nurturing were closely associated with [trees]. Hathor, Nut, and Isis appear frequently in the religious imagery and literature [in relation to trees]" (332).

Plants and flowers were also associated with the gods, and the flowers of the ished tree were known as "flowers of life" for their life-giving properties. Eternity, then, was not an ethereal, nebulous concept of some 'heaven' far from the earth but a daily encounter with the gods and goddesses one would continue to have contact with forever, in life and after death.

Hathor

In order for one to experience this kind of bliss, however, one needed to be aware of the importance of harmony in one's life and how a lack of such harmony affected others as well as one's self. The 'gateway sin' for the ancient Egyptians was ingratitude because it threw one off balance and allowed for every other sin to take root in a person's soul. Once one lost sight of what there was to be grateful for, one's thoughts and energies were drawn toward the forces of darkness and chaos. This belief gave rise to rituals such as The Five Gifts of Hathor in which one would consider the fingers of one's hand and name the five things in life one was most grateful for. One was encouraged to be specific in this, naming anything one held dear such as a spouse, one's children, one's dog or cat, or the tree by the stream in the yard. As one's hand was readily available at all times, it would serve as a reminder that there were always five things one should be grateful for, and this would help one to maintain a light heart in keeping with harmonious balance. This was important throughout one's life and remained equally significant after one's death since, in order to progress on toward an eternal life of bliss, one's heart needed to be lighter than a feather when one stood in judgment before Osiris.

The Soul & The Hall of Truth

According to the scholar Margaret Bunson:
The Egyptians feared eternal darkness and unconsciousness in the afterlife because both conditions belied the orderly

transmission of light and movement evident in the universe. They understood that death was the gateway to eternity. The Egyptians thus esteemed the act of dying and venerated the structures and the rituals involved in such a human adventure. The structures of the dead can still be seen throughout Egypt in the modern day in the tombs and pyramids which still rise from the landscape. There were structures and rituals after life, however, which were just as important.

The soul was thought to consist of nine separate parts: the Khat was the physical body; the Ka one's double-form; the Ba a human-headed bird aspect which could speed between earth and the heavens; Shuyet was the shadow self; Akh the immortal, transformed self, Sahu and Sechem aspects of the Akh; Ab was the heart, the source of good and evil; Ren was one's secret name. All nine of these aspects were part of one's earthly existence and, at death, the Akh (with the Sahu and Sechem) appeared before the great god Osiris in the Hall of Truth and in the presence of the Forty-Two Judges to have one's heart (Ab) weighed in the balance on a golden scale against the white feather of truth.

One would need to recite the Negative Confession (a list of those sins one could honestly claim one had not committed in life) and then one's heart was placed on the scale. If one's heart was lighter than the feather, one waited while Osiris conferred with the Forty-Two Judges and the god of wisdom, Thoth, and, if considered worthy, was allowed to pass on through the hall and continue one's existence in paradise; if one's heart was heavier than the feather it was thrown to the floor where it was devoured by the monster Ammut (the gobbler), and one then ceased to exist.

Weighing the Heart, Book of the Dead
Once through the Hall of Truth, one was then guided to the boat of Hraf-haf ("He Who Looks Behind Him"), an unpleasant creature, always cranky and offensive, whom one had to find some way to be kind and courteous to. By showing kindness to the unkind Hraf-haf, one showed one was worthy to be ferried across the waters of Lily Lake (also known as The Lake of Flowers) to the Field of Reeds which was a mirror image of one's life on earth except there was no disease, no disappointment, and no death. One would then continue one's existence just as before, awaiting those one loved in life to pass over themselves or meeting those who had gone on before.

The Clergy, Temples & Scripture
Although the Greek historian Herodotus claims that only men could be priests in ancient Egypt, the Egyptian record argues otherwise. Women could be priests of the cult of their goddess from the Old Kingdom onward and were accorded the same respect as their male counterparts. Usually a member of the clergy had to be of the same sex as the deity they served. The cult of Hathor, most notably, was routinely attended to by female clergy (it should be noted that 'cult' did not have the same meaning in ancient Egypt that it does today. Cults were simply sects of one religion). Priests and Priestesses could marry, have children, own land and homes and lived as anyone else except for certain ritual practices and observances regarding purification before officiating. Bunson writes:
In most periods, the priests of Egypt were members of a family long connected to a particular cult or temple. Priests recruited new members from among their own clans, generation after generation. This meant that they did not live apart from their own people and thus maintained an awareness of the state of affairs in their communities (209).

Priests, like scribes, went through a prolonged training period before beginning service and, once ordained, took care of the temple or temple complex, performed rituals and observances (such as marriages, blessings on a home or project, funerals), performed the duties of doctors, healers, astrologers, scientists, and psychologists, and also interpreted dreams. They blessed amulets to ward off demons or increase fertility, and also performed exorcisms and purification rites to rid a home of ghosts. Their chief duty was to the god they served and the people of the community, and an important part of that duty was their care of the temple and the statue of the god within. Priests were also doctors in the service of Heka, no matter what other deity they served directly. An example of this is how all the priests and priestesses of the goddess Serket (Selket) were doctors but their ability to heal and invoke Serket was enabled through the power of Heka.

The temples of ancient Egypt were thought to be the literal homes of the deities they honored. Every morning the head priest or priestess, after purifying themselves with a bath and dressing in clean white linen and clean sandals, would enter the temple and attend to the statue of the god as they would to a person they were charged to care for. The doors of the sanctuary were opened to let in the morning light, and the statue, which always resided in the innermost sanctuary, was cleaned, dressed, and anointed with oil; afterwards, the sanctuary doors were closed and locked. No one but the head priest was allowed such close contact with the god. Those who came to the temple to worship only were allowed in the outer areas where they were met by lesser clergy who addressed their needs and accepted their offerings.

Egyptian Temple

There were no official `scriptures' used by the clergy but the concepts conveyed at the temple are thought to have been similar to those found in works such as the Pyramid Texts, the later Coffin Texts, and the spells found in the Egyptian Book of the Dead. Although the Book of the Dead is often referred to as `The Ancient Egyptian Bible' it was no such thing. The Book of the Dead is a collection of spells for the soul in the afterlife. The Pyramid Texts are the oldest religious texts in ancient Egypt dating from c. 2400-2300 BCE. The Coffin Texts were developed later from the Pyramid Texts c. 2134-2040 BCE while the Book of the Dead (actually known as the Book on Coming Forth by Day) was set down sometime c. 1550-1070 BCE.

All three of these works deal with how the soul is to navigate the afterlife. Their titles (given by European scholars) and the number of grand tombs and statuary throughout Egypt, not to mention the elaborate burial rituals and mummies, have led many people to conclude that Egypt was a culture obsessed with death when, actually, the Egyptians were wholly concerned with life. The Book on Coming Forth by Day, as well as the earlier texts, present spiritual truths one would have heard while in life and remind the soul of how one should now act in the next phase of one's existence without a physical body or a material world. The soul of any Egyptian was expected to recall these truths from life, even if they never set foot inside a temple compound, because of the many religious festivals the Egyptians enjoyed throughout the year.

Religious Festivals & Religious Life

Religious festivals in Egypt integrated the sacred aspect of the gods seamlessly with the daily lives of the people. Egyptian scholar Lynn Meskell notes that "religious festivals actualized belief; they were not simply social celebrations. They acted in a multiplicity of related spheres" (Nardo, 99). There were grand festivals such as The Beautiful Festival of the Wadi in honor of the god Amun and lesser festivals for other gods or to celebrate events in the life of the community.

Bunson writes, "On certain days, in some eras several times a month, the god was carried on arks or ships into the streets or set sail on the Nile. There the oracles took place and the priests answered petitions" (209). The statue of the god would be removed from the inner sanctuary to visit the members of the community and take part in the celebration; a custom which may have developed independently in Egypt or come from Mesopotamia where this practice had a long history.

The Beautiful Festival of the Wadi was a celebration of life, wholeness, and community, and, as Meskell notes, people attended this festival and visited the shrine to "pray for bodily integrity and physical vitality" while leaving offerings to the god or goddess as a sign of gratitude for their lives and health. Meskell writes:

One may envisage a priest or priestess coming and collecting the offerings and then replacing the baskets, some of which have been detected archaeologically. The fact that these items of jewelry were personal objects suggests a powerful and intimate link with the goddess. Moreover, at the shrine site of Timna in the Sinai, votives were ritually smashed to signify the handing over from human to deity, attesting to the range of ritual practices occurring at the time. There was a high proportion of female donors in the New Kingdom, although generally tomb paintings tend not to show the religous practices of women but rather focus on male activities (101).

The smashing of the votives signified one's surrender to the benevolent will of the gods. A votive was anything offered in fulfillment of a vow or in the hopes of attaining some wish. While votives were often left intact, they were sometimes ritually destroyed to signify the devotion one had to the gods; one was surrendering to them something precious which one could not take back.

There was no distinction at these festivals between those acts considered 'holy' and those which a modern sensibility would label 'profane'. The whole of one's life was open for exploration during a festival, and this included sexual activity, drunkenness, prayer, blessings for one's sex life, for one's family, for one's health, and offerings made both in gratitude and thanksgiving and in supplication.

Families attended the festivals together as did teenagers and young couples and those hoping to find a mate. Elder members of the community, the wealthy, the poor, the ruling class, and the slaves were all a part of the religious life of the community because their religion and their daily lives were completely intertwined and, through that faith, they recognized their individual lives were all an interwoven tapestry with every other.

Hymns and Prayers

The Egyptians produced numerous prayers and hymns, written in the form of poetry. Hymns and prayers follow a similar structure and are distinguished mainly by the purposes they serve. Hymns were written to praise particular deities. Like ritual texts, they were written on papyri and on temple walls, and they were probably recited as part of the rituals they accompany in temple inscriptions.

Most are structured according to a set literary formula, designed to expound on the nature, aspects, and mythological functions of a given deity. They tend to speak more explicitly about fundamental theology than other Egyptian religious writings, and became particularly important in the New Kingdom, a period of particularly active theological discourse. Prayers follow the same general pattern as hymns, but address the relevant god in a more personal way, asking for blessings, help, or forgiveness for wrongdoing. Such prayers are rare before the New Kingdom, indicating that in earlier periods such direct personal interaction with a deity was not believed possible, or at least was less likely to be expressed in writing. They are known mainly from inscriptions on statues and stelae left in sacred sites as votive offerings.

Legacy

Egyptian religion produced the temples and tombs which are ancient Egypt's most enduring monuments, but it also left many influences on other cultures. In pharaonic times many of its symbols, such as the sphinx and winged solar disk, spread widely across the Mediterranean and Near East, as did some of its deities, such as Bes. Some of these connections are difficult to trace. The Greek concept of Elysium may have derived from the Egyptian vision of the afterlife.

In late antiquity, the Christian conception of Hell was most likely influenced by some of the imagery of the Duat, and the iconography of Mary may have been influenced by that of Isis. Egyptian beliefs also influenced or gave rise to several esoteric belief systems developed by Greeks and Romans who saw Egypt as a source of mystic wisdom. Hermeticism, for instance, derived from the tradition of secret magical knowledge associated with Thoth.

Traces of ancient beliefs remained in Egyptian folk traditions into modern times, but its impact on modern societies greatly increased with the French Campaign in Egypt and Syria in 1798. As a result of it, Westerners began to study Egyptian beliefs firsthand, and Egyptian religious motifs were adopted into Western art. Egyptian religion has since had a significant impact on popular culture. Due to continued interest in Egyptian belief, in the late 20th century several new religious groups formed based on different reconstructions of ancient Egyptian religion.

Historical sources

Prehistory

When exactly early hominids first arrived in Egypt is unclear. The earliest migration of hominids out of Africa took place almost 2 million years ago, with modern humans dispersing out of Africa about 100,000 years ago. Egypt may have been used to reach Asia in some of these migrations.

Villages dependent on agriculture began to appear in Egypt about 7,000 years ago, and the civilization's earliest written inscriptions date back about 5,200 years; they discuss the early rulers of Egypt. These early rulers include Iry-Hor, who, according to recently discovered inscriptions, founded Memphis, a city that served as Egypt's capital for much of its history. When and how Egypt was united is unclear and is a matter of debate among archaeologists and historians.

Egypt's climate was much wetter in prehistoric times than it is today. This means that some areas that are now barren desert were fertile. One famous archaeological site where this can be seen is at the "cave of swimmers" (as it is called today) on the Gilf Kebir plateau in southwest Egypt. The cave is now surrounded by miles of barren desert; however, it has rock art showing what some scholars interpret as people swimming. The exact date of the rock art is unclear, although scholars think that it was created in prehistoric times.

Egypt's 30 dynasties

Egypt's history has traditionally been divided into 30 (sometimes 31) dynasties. This tradition started with the Egyptian priest Manetho, who lived during the third century B.C. His accounts of ancient Egyptian history were preserved by ancient Greek writers and, until the deciphering of hieroglyphic writing in the 19th century, were one of the few historical accounts that scholars could read.

Modern-day scholars often group these dynasties into several periods. Dynasties one and two date back around 5,000 years and are often called the "early dynastic" or "archaic" period. The first pharaoh of the first dynasty was a ruler named Menes (or Narmer, as he is called in Greek). He lived over 5,000 years ago, and while ancient writers sometimes credited him as being the first pharaoh of a united Egypt we know today that this is not true — there was a group of Egyptian rulers that predated Menes. Scholars sometimes refer to these pre-Menes rulers as being part of a "dynasty zero."

Dynasties 3-6 date from roughly 2650–2150 B.C. and are often lumped into a time period called the "Old Kingdom" by modern-day scholars. During this time pyramid building techniques were developed and the pyramids of Giza were built.

From 2150–2030 B.C. (a time period that encompassed dynasties 7-10 and part of the 11) the central government in Egypt was weak and the country was often controlled by different regional leaders. Why the Old Kingdom collapsed is a matter of debate among scholars, with recent research indicating that drought and climate change played a significant role. During this time other cities and civilizations in the Middle East also collapsed, with evidence at archaeological sites indicating that a period of drought and arid climate hit sites across the Middle East.

Dynasties 12, 13, as well as part of the 11th are often called the "Middle Kingdom" by scholars and lasted from ca. 2030–1640 B.C. At the start of this dynasty, a ruler named Mentuhotep II (who reigned until about 2000 B.C.) reunited Egypt into a single country. Pyramid building resumed in Egypt, and a sizable number of texts documenting the civilization's literature and science were recorded. Among the surviving texts is the Edwin Smith surgical papyrus, which includes a variety of medical treatments that modern-day medical doctors have hailed as being advanced for their time.

Dynasties 14-17 are often lumped into the "second intermediate period" by modern-day scholars. During this time central government again collapsed in Egypt, with part of the country being occupied by the "Hyksos" a group from the Levant (an area that encompasses modern-day Israel, Palestine, Lebanon, Jordan and Syria). One gruesome find from this time period is a series of severed hands, cut off from their human victims, which were found at a palace at the city of Avaris, the capital of Hyksos-controlled Egypt. The cut-off hands may have been presented by soldiers to a ruler in exchange for gold.

Scholars often refer to dynasties 18-20 as encompassing the "New Kingdom," a period that lasted ca. 1550–1070 B.C. This time period takes place after the Hyksos had been driven out of Egypt by a series of Egyptian rulers and the country was reunited. Perhaps the most famous archaeological site from this time period is the Valley of the Kings, which holds the burial sites of many Egyptian rulers from this time period, including that of Tutankhamun (reign ca. 1336–1327 B.C.), whose rich tomb was found intact. [Photos: More Than 40 Tombs Discovered in Upper Egypt]

Dynasties 21-24 (a period from ca. 1070–713 B.C.) are often called the "third intermediate period" by modern-day scholars. The central government was sometimes weak during this time period and the country was not always united. During this time cities and civilizations across the Middle East had been destroyed by a wave of people from the Aegean, whom modern-day scholars sometimes call the "Sea Peoples." While Egyptian rulers claimed to have defeated the Sea Peoples in battle, it didn't prevent Egyptian civilization from also collapsing. The loss of trade routes and revenue may have played a role in the weakening of Egypt's central government.

Dynasties 25-31 (date ca. 712–332 B.C.) are often referred to as the "late period" by scholars. Egypt was sometimes under the control of foreign powers during this period. The rulers of the 25th dynasty were from Nubia, an area now located in southern Egypt and northern Sudan. The Persians and Assyrians also controlled Egypt at different times during the late period.

In 332 B.C. Alexander the Great drove the Persians out of Egypt and incorporated the country into the Macedonian Empire. After Alexander the Great's death, a line of rulers descended from Ptolemy Soter, one of Alexander's generals. The last of these "Ptolemaic" rulers (as scholars often call them) was Cleopatra VII, who committed suicide in 30 B.C after the defeat of her forces by the Roman emperor Augustus at the Battle of Actium. After her death, Egypt was incorporated into the Roman Empire.

Although the Roman emperors were based in Rome, the Egyptians treated them as pharaohs. One recently excavated carving shows the emperor Claudius (reign A.D. 41-54) dressed as a pharaoh. The carving has hieroglyphic inscriptions that say that Claudius is the "Son of Ra, Lord of the Crowns," and is "King of Upper and Lower Egypt, Lord of the Two Lands."

Neither the Ptolemaic or Roman rulers are considered to be part of a numbered dynasty.

Origins

The religious life of the ancient Egyptians spans a period of three thousand years beginning c. 3100 B.C.E. and includes a wide array of gods who enjoyed periods of development, longevity and prominence. The standard explanation concerning their origin suggests that the earliest gods were based on the forces of nature. Animism, the idea that spirits inhabit various features of the natural world, such as the spirits of the river, the sun and the wind, gradually took on more character as the spirits developed into personified gods in the collective imagination of the people. Other scholars disagree, given that there is evidence of gods being worshiped from the earliest stages of Egyptian civilization.

Ancient Egyptians believed in many gods who performed a variety of specific functions. Their involvement in daily life was critical to existence itself, since the gods were responsible for the maintenance of the universe. The complex religious practices that grew out of this concept thrived in Egypt for millennia.

A Plethora of Gods

Although gods and goddesses tended to rise from localities, belief in them was not restricted to certain geographic areas. Nor was it common for people to be devotees of particular deities. In fact, according to Emily Teeter from the University of Chicago, and Douglas Brewer from the University of Illinois, as religious and concepts developed and took new forms over the course of time, they tended to layer in a complex religious system rather than discard old ideas for new ones. As a result, there were numerous gods who performed a variety of functions. It was possible for an average Egyptian to call on many of them at one time.

Ancient Egyptians believed in many gods who performed a variety of specific functions. Their involvement in daily life was critical to existence itself, since the gods were responsible for the maintenance of the universe. The complex religious practices that grew out of this concept thrived in Egypt for millennia.

Kings and Temple Worship

Statues of gods were made to worship and appease, and worshipers ritually provided sacrifice for the gods to win their protection and help in preserving order. The king was regarded as the high priest, with the responsibility to appease the gods. Usually the king did not participate in person. Priests stood in his place in front of the statues that were believed to be physical homes for the gods. In return, the king's own divinity was granted to him by the gods. But famine, drought or pestilence were seen by the people as the results of the displeasure of a god. Due to this concept, the gods were invoked and appeased often throughout the day, playing a major role in the daily lives of ancient Egyptians.

Ancient Egyptians believed in many gods who performed a variety of specific functions. Their involvement in daily life was critical to existence itself, since the gods were responsible for the maintenance of the universe. The complex religious practices that grew out of this concept thrived in Egypt for millennia.

Daily Life

According to the religious system of ancient Egypt, the gods not only protected and provided for the people, but were systemically involved in maintaining the order of daily life. The word "maat," represented and personified by the god Maat, referred to the order and balance of the universe. The march of the sun across the sky, the flow of the river Nile, the growth of food and all other aspects of life were seen as immediate results of the gods' involvement in ordering the cosmos.

CHAPTER 3

COSMOLOGY

The Egyptian conception of the universe centered on Ma'at, a word that encompasses several concepts in English, including "truth," "justice," and "order." It was the fixed, eternal order of the universe, both in the cosmos and in human society. It had existed since the creation of the world, and without it the world would lose its cohesion. In Egyptian belief, Ma'at was constantly under threat from the forces of disorder, so all of society was required to maintain it.

On the human level this meant that all members of society should cooperate and coexist; on the cosmic level it meant that all of the forces of nature - the gods - should continue to function in balance. This latter goal was central to Egyptian religion. The Egyptians sought to maintain Ma'at in the cosmos by sustaining the gods through offerings and by performing rituals which staved off disorder and perpetuated the cycles of nature.

The most important part of the Egyptian view of the cosmos was the conception of time, which was greatly concerned with the maintenance of Ma'at. Throughout the linear passage of time, a cyclical pattern recurred, in which Ma'at was renewed by periodic events which echoed the original creation. Among these events were the annual Nile flood and the succession from one king to another, but the most important was the daily journey of the sun god Ra.

When envisioning the shape of the cosmos, the Egyptians saw the earth as a flat expanse of land, personified by the god Geb, over which arched the sky goddess Nut. The two were separated by Shu, the god of air. Beneath the earth lay a parallel underworld and undersky, and beyond the skies lay the infinite expanse of Nu, the chaos that had existed before creation. The Egyptians also believed in a place called the Duat, a mysterious region associated with death and rebirth, that may have lain in the underworld or in the sky. Each day, Ra traveled over the earth across the underside of the sky, and at night he passed through the Duat to be reborn at dawn.

In Egyptian belief, this cosmos was inhabited by three types of sentient beings. One was the gods; another was the spirits of deceased humans, who existed in the divine realm and possessed many of the gods' abilities. Living humans were the third category, and the most important among them was the pharaoh, who bridged the human and divine realms.

The Egyptian universe centered on Ma'at, which has several meanings in English, including truth, justice and order. It was fixed and eternal (without it the world would fall apart), and there were constant threats of disorder requiring society to work to maintain it. Inhabitants of the cosmos included the gods, the spirits of deceased humans, and living humans, the most important of which was the pharaoh. Humans should cooperate to achieve this, and gods should function in balance. Ma'at was renewed by periodic events, such as the annual Nile flood, which echoed the original creation. Most important of these was the daily journey of the sun god Ra.

Egyptians saw the earth as flat land (the god Geb), over which arched the sky (goddess Nut); they were separated by Shu, the god of air. Underneath the earth was a parallel underworld and undersky, and beyond the skies lay Nu, the chaos before creation. Duat was a mysterious area associated with death and rebirth, and each day Ra passed through Duat after traveling over the earth during the day.

PART 2 – MAJOR MYTHS
CHAPTER 4

MYTHS

Many of the Egyptian myths focus on origin. From the origin of the world, natural phenomena and even some of the human institutions. Even kingship was said to originate with the gods and it is then passed on to the human Pharaohs. Warfare was said to originate when the sun god Ra withdrew in to the sky, then the humans began to fight among each other.

Maat refers to order and is believed to have been established at the creation of the world from the chaos. Maat also refers to the normal patterns and behavior of natural phenomena as well as that of humans. When maat exists, life and happiness becomes possible.

Egyptian gods govern the all the forces of nature as per the myths and thus are responsible for life and the correct functioning of everything in existence. The human responsible for maat among the people is the Pharaoh and in the myths, pharaoh is the son of various gods and represents them on earth. He is also responsible in seeing to the rituals necessary to keep the gods happy.

Egyptian Myths

As in most myths, the Egyptian mythology focuses around traditions, daily life as well as the big questions such as the fate of the universe. Egyptian gods relate to physical objects such as the sun and the earth as well as more abstract forces such as creativity and knowledge.

The Egyptians believed that their gods were the power behind all forces and elements. The myths are often incomplete or even only partial narratives, and tend to be quite flexible. Some of the myths even seem to contradict each other, but this could also be due to varied religious ideas and practices in different regions of Egypt at the time.

Many areas based their religion around a patron god and adapted the myths to suit their cults. The Egyptians also combined and adapted many myths and combined old myths with new ones, making their tales and deities very complicated.

Some of the fundamental myths focus on the shape of the world, in this case a flat piece of land (personified as the god Geb), over which is the sky (the goddess Nut). Sky and earth as separated by air (Shu) and the sun (Ra) travels across the sky and then disappears in to the Duat (an area on the border of the formless water that earth was brought from (personified by the god Nun)). Egypt was seen as the center of the world and most myths are told of the gods being in Egypt, very seldom in a foreign setting.

Creation myths are many and some are similar while others are not but most have a few elements in common. Most myths agree that the world came from the waters of chaos (Nu) and that a pyramid (benben) was the first thing to arise from the waters.

The sun was said to arise from this first mound either directly or a lotus flower and originally in the form of a child, a falcon, a scarab beetle or a heron. The origin of humans is not as well documented in the myths except for the myths which say humans came from the tears of Ra-Atum or Eye of Ra or molded from clay by Khnum. Most myths are around creationism from chaos rather than human beginnings.

CREATION

The Egyptian creation myths are a series of ancient accounts concerning the origins of the sun, earth, moon and stars as well as the creation of life. While there are many variations on the myth, the one originating at Heliopolis -- one of the oldest cities along the Nile -- is perhaps the most well-known. The story tells of several deities and the role each played in creation. Ra, the god of the sun, is the primary deity in the myth, but other gods, including Khnum and Nut, play a part. The Egyptian creation myth takes place over a period of seven days, similar to the Hebrew creation story.

Sources of the Myths
Most of the information on the Egyptian creation myths comes from pyramid texts, tomb wall decorations and writings dating back to the Old Kingdom (2780 - 2250 B.C.). The different creation stories are associated with the cult of a particular deity in the major cities -- Hermopolis, Heliopolis, Memphis and Thebes. Heliopolis was the center of worship of the sun god Ra. Ancient Egyptian religion was polytheistic, having many gods that existed in a hierarchy; Ra was believed to be the most powerful of the gods. The myths recount eight primordial deities called the Ogdoad and they make reference to a god called Atum who willed himself into being. Many gods appear in artwork from the Early Dynastic Period (3000 - 2575 B.C.), but a more important source is the non-religious literature that began to appear in the Middle Kingdom. Several works completely recount earlier creation narratives. An early educational text called "Teaching for King Merykara" from

the Middle Kingdom references the Heliopolis myth, and the earliest known short story, "Tale of the Shipwrecked Sailor," reconceptualizes many of the gods' characteristics.

The Egyptian creation myths are a series of ancient accounts concerning the origins of the sun, earth, moon and stars as well as the creation of life. While there are many variations on the myth, the one originating at Heliopolis -- one of the oldest cities along the Nile -- is perhaps the most well-known. The story tells of several deities and the role each played in creation. Ra, the god of the sun, is the primary deity in the myth, but other gods, including Khnum and Nut, play a part. The Egyptian creation myth takes place over a period of seven days, similar to the Hebrew creation story.

Commonalities Between Myths

While these differing creation stories competed to some extent, in other ways they are complementary, representing different aspects of the overall Egyptian understanding of creation. All of the stories hold that the world arose from a lifeless water of chaos, called Nu. A benben, or pyramid-shaped mound, is the first element to emerge from Nu. This was likely inspired by the flooding of the Nile each year. All of the myths also have as their central figure Ra, the sun god. Another common element is the figure of a "cosmic egg," a life-giving egg that in some myths birthed Ra and in others emerged from the chaotic Nu.

The Egyptian creation myths are a series of ancient accounts concerning the origins of the sun, earth, moon and stars as well as the creation of life. While there are many variations on the myth, the one originating at Heliopolis -- one of the oldest cities along the Nile -- is perhaps the most well-known. The story tells of several deities and the role each played in creation. Ra, the god of the sun, is the primary deity in the myth, but other gods, including Khnum and Nut, play a part. The Egyptian creation myth takes place over a period of seven days, similar to the Hebrew creation story.

Atum and Mythical Theology
In Heliopolis, the creation of the world is attributed to Atum, a god so closely identified with Ra that he would become known as Atum-Ra. Atum is thought to have exited from Nu as an inert potential being until he willed himself into existence. Atum's power was so great that he was thought to have been the source of all the elements and natural forces in the universe. Atum also created the air god Shu and his sister Tefnut who would later give birth to the earth god Geb and the sky goddess Nut. In turn, Geb and Nut have four children, each representing a force of life. Osiris is the god of fertility and regeneration; Isis is the goddess of motherhood; Set is the god of male sexuality; and Nephthys is the goddess of female sexuality. In totality, Atum's "family" of gods and goddesses represents the process by which life is made possible. Together the nine deities are called the Ennead.

The Egyptian creation myths are a series of ancient accounts concerning the origins of the sun, earth, moon and stars as well as the creation of life. While there are many variations on the myth, the one originating at Heliopolis -- one of the oldest cities along the Nile -- is perhaps the most well-known. The story tells of several deities and the role each played in creation. Ra, the god of the sun, is the primary deity in the myth, but other gods, including Khnum and Nut, play a part. The Egyptian creation myth takes place over a period of seven days, similar to the Hebrew creation story.

Comparison to the Hebrew Myth
The Egyptian creation myth at Heliopolis was historically developed before the Hebrew creation story found in the Bible, but there are many similarities between the two stories. Both myths concern nature and the creation of human beings, and both take place over a period of seven days. The Egyptian story takes the Nile River as its cosmic starting place. Water is considered the primary element for life that existed before anything else. This element of the story was passed to the Hebrews and adapted to their own myth. However, while the Egyptians believed in many gods, the Hebrew story is essentially monotheistic.

ANCIENT EGYPTIAN CREATION MYTHS

Egyptian myths are the basis of ancient tradition, but also address profound questions about the nature of disorder and the fate of the Universe. Egyptian deities represent both physical objects like the earth and Sun, and more abstract forces such as knowledge and creativity. Actions of the Gods, along with their own interactions control all of forces and elements.
Most of Egypt's gods, do not feature strongly in written mythology. However, their nature and relationships with other deities are often established in lists or short statements. When Egyptian gods are included, the narratives point out their important role in the cosmos. Although mythology is a major element in Egyptian religious understanding, it is not as important as other cultures. Egyptian myths sometimes use symbolism to help us understand life in this realm.
Few complete stories appear in the sources for Egyptian mythological and are often contain portions of a larger story. Their importance lies in their meaning, rather than their value

as stories. Egyptian stories were also very flexible and often conflict with another. One suggested reason for this is that religious ideas differed over time and between regions. There were lots of local cults based around patron gods. Instead of lengthy, fixed narratives, Egyptian mythology is both flexible and avoids dogma. Only a small proportion of material has survived to the present, and not equally abundant in all periods, so beliefs in some eras is more poorly understood than others.

This is a list of available sources for Egyptian mythology: -
Artwork from the Early Dynastic Period of Egypt's history (c. 3100–2686 BC)
The Pyramid Texts is a collection of several hundred incantations inscribed in the interiors of pyramids from the 24th century BC. These are funerary texts to ensure kings buried in the pyramid would pass through to the afterlife. Many of these texts are much older than their first known written copies, and provide details of the early stages of Egyptian religious belief.
The Coffin Texts from the First Intermediate Period (c. 2181–2055 BC), which contain similar material to The Pyramid Texts and also available to non-royals.
Book of the Dead is a funerary text used from the beginning of the New Kingdom (c. 1550 BC) up to c. 50 BC.
Books of Breathing from the Late Period (664–323 BC) were developed out of earlier collections.
Texts such as the Amduat, the Book of Gates, and the Book of Caverns from The New Kingdom contain detailed descriptions of the journey of the sun god.
Temple remains which mostly date from the New Kingdom and later, contain libraries, storing papyri of both hymns

(which often refer to myths) and religious rituals. The decorated temples themselves also a rich source of myth.

Greek and Roman writings by Herodotus, Diodorus Siculus, Plutarch and others. Their knowledge was limited because they were forbidden from many religious practices. Also, statements about Egyptian beliefs were affected by their own bias against Egypt's culture.

THE REIGN OF THE SUN GOD "RA"

In the period of the mythic past after the creation, Ra dwells on earth as king of the gods and of humans. This period is the closest thing to a golden age in Egyptian tradition, the period of stability that the Egyptians constantly sought to evoke and imitate. Yet the stories about Ra's reign focus on conflicts between him and forces that disrupt his rule, reflecting the king's role in Egyptian ideology as enforcer of Ma'at.

In an episode known in different versions from temple texts, some of the gods defy Ra's authority, and he destroys them with the help and advice of other gods like Thoth and Horus the Elder. At one point he faces dissent even from an extension of himself, the Eye of Ra, which can act independently of him in the form of a goddess. The Eye goddess becomes angry with Ra and runs away from him, wandering wild and dangerous in the lands outside Egypt. Weakened by her absence, Ra sends one of the other gods - Shu, Thoth, or Anhur, in different accounts - to retrieve her, by force or persuasion. Because the Eye of Ra is associated with the star Sothis, whose heliacal rising signaled the start of the Nile flood, the return of the Eye goddess to Egypt coincides with the life-giving inundation. Upon her return, the goddess becomes the consort of Ra or of the god who has retrieved her. Her pacification restores order and renews life.

As Ra grows older and weaker, humanity, too, turns against him. In an episode often called "The Destruction of Mankind", related in The Book of the Heavenly Cow, Ra discovers that humanity is plotting rebellion against him and sends his Eye to punish them. She slays many people, but Ra apparently decides that he does not want her to destroy all of humanity. He has beer dyed red to resemble blood and spreads it over the field. The Eye goddess drinks the beer, becomes drunk, and ceases her rampage. Ra then withdraws into the sky, weary of ruling on earth, and begins his daily journey through the heavens and the Duat. The surviving humans are dismayed, and they attack the people among them who plotted against Ra. This event is the origin of warfare, death, and humans' constant struggle to protect Ma'at from the destructive actions of other people.

In The Book of the Heavenly Cow, the results of the destruction of mankind seem to mark the end of the direct reign of the gods and of the linear time of myth. The beginning of Ra's journey is the beginning of the cyclical time of the present. Yet in other sources, mythic time continues after this change. Egyptian accounts give sequences of divine rulers who take the place of the sun god as king on earth, each reigning for many thousands of years. Although accounts differ as to which gods reigned and in what order, the succession from Ra-Atum to his descendants Shu and Geb - in which the kingship passes to the male in each generation of the Ennead - is common. Both of them face revolts that parallel those in the reign of the sun god, but the revolt that receives the most attention in Egyptian sources is the one in the reign of Geb's heir Osiris.

CHAPTER 5

OSIRIS MYTH

Osiris, one of Egypt's most important deities, was god of the underworld. He also symbolized death, resurrection, and the cycle of Nile floods that Egypt relied on for agricultural fertility.
According to the myth, Osiris was a king of Egypt who was murdered and dismembered by his brother Seth. His wife, Isis, reassembled his body and resurrected him, allowing them to conceive a son, the god Horus. He was represented as a mummified king, wearing wrappings that left only the green skin of his hands and face exposed.
Osiris was originally a vegetation god linked with the growth of crops. He was the mythological first king of Egypt and one of the most important of the gods. It was thought that he brought civilization to the race of mankind. He was murdered by his brother Seth, brought back to life by his wife Isis, and went on to become the ruler of the underworld and judge of the dead.
He is usually depicted as a mummy holding the crook and flail of kingship. On his head he wears the white crown of Upper Egypt flanked by two plumes of feathers. Sometimes he is shown with the horns of a ram. His skin is depicted as blue, the color of the dead; black, the color of the fertile earth; or green, representing resurrection.
Osiris was an ancient corn-deity who followers, who came probably from Syria, identified their god with a pastoral deity called Andjeti and established themselves in his Delta city in

predynastic times. The cult object, or fetish, known as the djed column and thought to represent four pillars seen one behind the other, or a man's backbone, or more probably a leafless cedar, was brought from Syria after which came the name of the city of Djedu. The city was subsequently renamed Per-Usire or Busiris after Usire, the Egyptian form of Osiris' name. Although, the meaning of this name is uncertain, it has been interpreted as "to create a throne" and as Seat or Power of the Eye.

The Osiris fertility cult soon spread, apparently peacefully, to many parts of Egypt. The god's associations with burial rites were also established early, because by the Fifth Dynasty he had absorbed the funerary gods of Abydos and dead pharaohs were identified with him. Since the funerary aspect ultimately became paramount, Osiris became the supreme god of Egypt. However, when speculating about the beliefs concerning the "First Time" when Osiris was incorporated by mythology into the Heliopolitan Ennead, it is easy to imagine the vegetation god being the son of Geb, the earth god.

Plutarch, in his treatise, present a fairly complete account of the Osiris myth with its accuracy confirmed by certain details in the Pyramid Texts and other documents of an earlier date. Accordingly Nut gave birth to Osiris at Thebes on the first of the five intercalary days that Thoth created for Nut because he was in love with her. At the birth of Osiris a voice was heard in the temple crying that the great and good king was born, or that the lord of all was entering the light. Re acknowledged Osiris as his heir, and at times is said to have begotten both Osiris and Horus, Thoth fathered Isis, and Geb only Seth (Set) and Nephthys. Also, according to legend, Osiris and Isis fell in love while still in the womb and then produced Horus the Elder. They were later married and Osiris succeeded his father Geb on the throne.

According to the First Time legends concerning Osiris the people of that time were barbarous cannibals. It was Osirs who instructed in the ways of civilization, teaching them what to eat and the methods of agriculture. He taught the proper worship of the gods, and drew up laws for them. Thoth helped by serving as Osiris' scribe, as well as inventing the arts and sciences, and naming things. Osiris governed by persuasion, not by force; and when having civilized Egypt by these methods, he decided to teach the rest of the world. He left Isis as regent during his absence. Osiris took with him on his mission many musicians and minor gods. Through arguments and hymn singing he persuaded other peoples of the things that he had taught his own people. However, during his absence Isis administered his kingdom, assisted by Thoth, but she was hard pressed by the tactics of Seth who not only coveted the throne, but also was enamored of her, and sought to change the order of things.

Not long after Osiris returned Seth, assisted by the queen of Ethiopia, Aso, and seventy-two conspirators, was determined to do away with him. Their plot was successful as Osiris fell to the conspirators, and it was Seth who cast his body into the floodwaters of the Nile. Isis sought and found the body of her husband, and with her own magical powers, assisted by Thoth, Nephthys, Ambis, and Horus, restored Osiris to life. But Osiris already belonged to the world of the dead, though after his resurrection he could have resumed the throne, but it is thought he preferred to maintain his kingdom in the land of the dead, leaving his earthly vindication in the hands of his posthumous son Horus.

The proceeding is just one of many versions of the Osiris myth. The legend of Osiris, perhaps more than the legend of any other god, has constantly undergone change throughout history. Obviously there are probable reasons for this: in earlier times, certainly, he was a subsidiary god in the national religion; originally his myth did not belong to any of the great cosmogonic systems, but was subordinated to the family of gods venerated at Heliopolis, Hermopolis, Memphis, and Thebes. The priests of these centers, anxious lest the ever-popular Osiris cult should swamp their own cults, accepted the fait accompli of gods combined into one human family by popular imagination. And in this family Sethting the Osiris myth gained widespread appeal. The suffering Osiris, head of an ideal family and model king, ultimately became the most important member of the divine family. By acquiring such veneration among worshipers, it is easily to understand how the cult of Osiris emerged.

The Osiris myth, perhaps related to the reign of some king, apparently absorbed the local Delta gods and unified Lower and Middle Egypt. As god of the dead, Osiris his greatest popularity; though he seemed to have begun his mythic career. But, gradually his worshipers hoped for an eternal happy life in the Underworld ruled but a just and good king. The location of this kingdom was thought to be either beneath Nun, or in the northern heavens, or in the west, and it was a gentle, fertile land.

As god of the dead, Osiris retained his earlier associations with the fertility of land and agriculture, and his death was identified with the dwindling of the Nile while his resurrection was associated with the flooding of it; the sun too, with its daily death and rebirth, became associated with Osiris. The rivalry with his brother Seth was view as the eternal opposition between the fertile Nile and the hostile desert, between life and death.

Osiris became worshipped throughout Egypt, usually as a triad that included Isis and Horus, his posthumous son. The chief cult centers were Busirs, representing his early home in the

Delta; Abydos, in Middle Egypt; and near Nedit, the center for the cult of the dead because it was thought to be the location where he was killed or where Isis found his body. Here Osiris was known as the "First of the Westerners," a title taken from the first god of Abydos, Khenti-Amentiu, which means King of the Dead. Starting in the Old Kingdom, the pharaohs were buried in Abydos, later notables and others too were buried or had their funeral stales there. Later Abydo became the center to which most Egyptians made pilgrimages, sometimes in proxy, then as part of their funeral ceremonies. A.G.H.

CHAPTER 6

THE JOURNEY OF THE SUN GOD

Ra is the most famous of the ancient Egyptian gods. He was a sun god who was the king of the ancient Egyptian pantheon and the creator of all life. He was the most widely worshipped god in ancient Egypt. Understanding his role in ancient Egyptian religion and how he was combined with other Egyptian gods over time can be difficult.

The sun, and therefore Ra, represented life, warmth, and growth to ancient Egyptians. He was so important that he earned the status of King of the Gods, with the Egyptian kings or pharaohs holding the title "sons of Ra."

Reference to Ra was first made during the Second Dynasty of ancient Egypt (c. 2890 – c. 2686 BC), also known as the Old Kingdom. His stature grew to that of a major god by the Fifth Dynasty (c. 2494 – c. 2345 BC).

Understanding and describing Ra is difficult because of the many forms he was depicted in, as well as the practice of creating new deities by merging existing deities. As one of the creator gods, Ra created himself before his identity was combined with several other gods, including HORUS and Atum. This resulted in new names such as Ra-Horakhty and Atum-Ra.

The sun god was believed to travel across the sky in a solar bark with the sun on his head. He travelled through the underworld in a bark called Sektet (meaning "growing weaker") during the night, defending himself against and overcoming monsters such as the serpent Apophis. The prayers and the blessings of the living supposedly accompanied him together with the souls of the dead. In the morning he travelled in a bark called Matet (meaning "becoming stronger").

Ra is pictured and represented in many pieces of ancient Egyptian art found in temples, tombs, hieroglyphics, relics, and other relics. He was generally depicted in human form, most notably with a falcon head crowned with a sun disc; a sacred cobra called Uraeus encircled the disc. Sometimes his head also took the form of a ram or a beetle, depending on the deity with whom he merged.

As the god of sun, which is indeed a fire by the nature, Ra needed a boat to travel between the earth and the waters of Duat, the underworld, and the heaven. He had two boats; Mandjet, his boat for daytime travels and Mesektet, his boat for nighttime travels. According to the myths Ra was accompanied by many gods during his journeys by his boats. Horus was told to be captain of Ra's boats with Ma'at and Thoth beside him. Sia (intelligence), Heka (magic), Hu (command) and Geb were other gods accompanying him during these travels. Uputaut, the deity known as "the god who opens the paths", was told to join these deities at nights to provide Ra with guidance.

According to the belief, Ra was living on the earth at the beginning ruling the world but people started doubting his capability as their God. Ra's daughter, Goddess Hathor was considered as his Eye and Ra sent her to punish humans who questioned his capability. Ra moved and started to living on the sky after that. Egyptian people blamed themselves for when Ra left the earth and people behind and moved to the sky. Some other gods in Egyptian belief like Osiris acted in Ra's stead and human kings, pharaohs, took over the job from them as the time passed.

Egyptian pharaohs spent most of their money on sun temples during the Fifth Dynasty. They were specially aligned in Ra's honor. By the time the New Kingdom arrived (c. 1550 BC), the worship became more elaborate. Detailed texts describing Ra's journey on the sun boats were written on tomb walls, while hymns, prayers, and spells were created in acts of worship.

Ra's Appearance
Ra was usually depicted in human form. He had a falcon head which is crowned with a sun disc. This sun disc was encircled by a sacred cobra named Uraeus. Ra has also been depicted as a man with the head of a beetle and also a human man with the head of a ram. The ancients also depicted Ra in full species form such as a serpent, heron, bull, lion, cat, ram, hawk, beetle, phoenix and others. His main symbol, however, is the sun disk.

Ra Mythology
The ancient Egyptians believed that as the sun god, Ra's role was to sail across the heavens during the day in his boat called the "Barque of Millions of Years." In the morning when Ra emerged from the east, his boat was named, "Madjet" which meant "becoming strong." By the end of the day the boat was called, "Semektet" which meant "becoming weak." At the end of the day, it was believed that Ra died (swallowed by Nut) and sailed on to the underworld, leaving the moon in his place to light up the world. Ra was reborn at dawn the very next day. During his journey across the heavens during the day, he fought with his main enemy, an evil serpent named Apep, or also, The Lord of Chaos. In some stories, Ra, in the form of a cat named Mau, defeats the evil serpent, Apep. This is part of the reason why cats are so highly-revered in Egypt.

Ra created himself from the primordial chaos. He is also known as Re and Atum. His children are Shu, the God of Dry Air and Father of the Sky, and his twin sister Tefnut, the Goddess of Moisture and Wetness. As a lion-headed goddess, Tefnut is responsible for dew and freshness. Humans were created from Ra's tears.

Although Ra was highly revered and devoutly worshiped by the ancient Egyptians, there is a story to suggest he eventually grew weak. In the Legend of Ra, Isis and the Snake, as Ra grew old, he dribbled saliva. Isis knew that Ra's power was hidden in his secret name. Isis gathered Ra's saliva and created a snake out of it. She set the snake in Ra's path and it bit him. Isis wanted the power Ra had always enjoyed, but she knew she had to get him to tell her his secret name. Eventually, because of the pain he was in, Ra allowed Isis to "search through him" and in so doing, she healed him and Ra's power was transferred over to her.

The Tree of Life is an important religious symbol to the Egyptians. The Tree of Life was located within Ra's sun temple in Heliopolis and was considered sacred. The fruit that sprang from this tree was not available to humans, but only in aging-rituals reserved for pharaohs. The Tree of Life is also referred to as the mythical, sacred Ished tree. Eternal life came to those who ate the fruit from the Tree of Life.

Another important ancient Egyptian symbol connected to Ra is the "Bennu". Bennu is the name of the bird that represented Ra's soul. This bird is a phoenix and it was seated at the Tree of Life in Ra's Sun Temple in Heliopolis. Inside the temple, on top of an obelisk, sat the Benben Stone. This pyramid-shaped stone served as a beacon to Bennu and is also an important ancient Egyptian religious symbol.

Worship of the Sun God

Solar temples were built for Ra but did not contain a statue of the god. Instead, they were created to be open to the sunlight that Ra represented. The earliest known temple built in honor of Ra exists in Heliopolis (what is now a Cairo suburb). This solar temple is known as "Benu-Phoenix" and is believed to have been erected in the exact spot where Ra emerged into creation.

Although Ra dates back to the second dynasty, he is not the oldest of the Egyptian gods. It wasn't until the fifth dynasty that Ra became closely associated with the pharaoh. As the king and leader of Egypt, the pharaoh was seen as the human manifestation of Horus, so the two gods became connected. This new deity fusion was then referred to as "Ra-Horakhty" meaning Ra is Horus of the Horizon. Ra's relationship with other gods did not stop there. As the powerful creator of mankind and the sun god, he also became associated with Atum to make "Atum-Ra."

Fifth Dynasty and subsequent pharaohs were all known as "The son of Ra" and Ra became incorporated into every pharaoh's name from then onward. During the Middle Kingdom, the new deity, Amun-Ra was formed. Amun was one of the gods who formed the Ogdoad (the assembly of eight gods who represented eight elements of creation).

The New Kingdom brought new heights of worship to Ra. Many tombs in the Valley of the Kings portray depictions of Ra and his journey through the underworld. During this time, many solar temples were built.

Eye of Ra

Present in the ancient Egyptian mythology is the Eye of Ra, shown as the sun disk with two 'uraeus' cobras coiled around it, next to the white and red crowns of Upper and Lower Egypt.

Initially associated with Horus (similarly to the wadjet, the Eye of Horus), the Eye of Ra shifted positions in the myths, becoming both an extension of Ra's power and a separate entity altogether.

A major belief among ancient Egyptians was that Ra journeyed in a boat through the sky during the day and through the underworld at night. Know more about the importance of Ra in ancient Egypt as well as his appearance, myths and powers through these 10 interesting facts.

1. Ra was regarded as the supreme power in the cosmic universe

By 25th century BC, Ra became one of the most important deities in ancient Egypt. He was believed to rule all parts of the world: the sky, the earth and the underworld. He was thus the supreme power in the cosmic universe. His importance can be understood by several myths regarding him. One myth believed him to be the ruler of all Gods while according to another, he was the only God and all other deities were nothing more than mere aspects of him. During the New Kingdom of ancient Egypt (16th century BC to 11th century BC), the worship of Ra gained even more significance and this is proved by depictions of the God on the tombs from this era.

2. Ra was usually portrayed as a man with a head of a falcon

Ra was represented in a variety of forms. His most common portrayal was of a man with the head of a falcon, crowned with a shiny sun disc. This sun disc is encircled by a sacred cobra called Uraeus. In some other depictions, Ra is also shown as a man with the head of a beetle or a ram. The sun disk, Ra's symbol, remains constant in all these illustrations. Among other things, Ra was also pictured as a full-bodied ram, beetle, phoenix, heron, serpent, bull, cat or lion. Some myths about Ra mention that Ra amalgamated himself in other forms such as Khepri or a beetle in the morning, Horakthty or solar disc in the noon and as Khnum or Atum (ram headed man) during sunset. At different times of the day, Ra changed from form to another but he continued to symbolize the sun throughout.

3. *Human beings were created by the tears of ra*

A common feature in Egyptian creation myths was of the world emerging from the waters of chaos that surround it. There are numerous creation myths of ancient Egypt and as Ra gained in significance, he too features in some of them. In one of the myths, Ra, being one of the creator gods, rose from the ocean of chaos on the primeval hill. He then created eight other gods. This thus produced the group of nine major deities in Egyptian mythology known as the Great Ennead. According to another myth, Ra was once roaming around the world and saw that everything was perfect, the sight brought tears to his eyes. The tears that fell on the earth became human beings.

4. *Ra journeyed through the sky during the day and through the underworld at night*

According to Egyptian mythology, Ra sailed across the heavens during the day time in his boat which they called the "Barque of Millions of Years". In the morning, this boat was called Madjet which means "becoming strong" while as the day ended, this boat was called Semektet which means "becoming weak". It was believed that Ra died after the day ended as he was swallowed by Nut, the goddess of the sky. After his death, Ra sailed across the underworld and the job of lighting up the world was left to the moon. During his journey through the underworld, Ra was attacked by Apep, a deity who was a giant serpent. However, Seth, the Egyptian god of chaos and disorder, accompanied Ra and defeated Apep to save Ra. As another day starts, Ra's voyage reaches its completion and he is reborn to begin his journey once again.

5. Ra was often combined with other prominent deities like horus and amun

Ra was often combined with other god in ancient Egyptian mythology. Ra was combined with Amun, another major Egyptian deity, to create the all powerful Amun-Ra, a solar creator god. At one time, Amun-Ra was given the official title "king of the gods". Atum, another major solar deity, was combined with Ra to form Atum-Ra. Horus was the sky god who was the most important deity before the rise of Ra during the Fifth Dynasty. He was combined with Ra to form Ra-Horakhty, which means 'Horus in the Horizon'. Khepri, a scarab beetle, was seen as the morning manifestation of Ra while Khnum, the ram-headed god, was seen as the evening manifestation of Ra. At noon, Ra was at his most powerful and was not combined with any other gods but known simply as Ra.

6. The eye of ra is an extension of his powers

The Eye of Ra is a symbol which was highly valued by ancient Egyptians. There are many myths about the Eye of Ra. According to one prominent myth, Ra's children Shu and Tefnut were going somewhere when they lost their way and could not be found. Ra plucked his eye out and sent it to look for his children. The eye found the two children and brought them back to their father. However, meanwhile Ra grew another eye. Seeing this new eye, his previous eye felt betrayed and came in a fit of rage. To calm it down, Ra gave the eye a powerful position on his forehead in the form of the uraeus, the emblematic cobra that appears frequently in

Egyptian art. The Eye of Ra became an extension of Ra's power serving as his feminine counterpart and a violent force that subdued his enemies.

7. He was the most powerful deity

In Egyptian mythology, Ra was the supreme power in the universe. According to several myths, he is the head of the Egyptian pantheon and ruler of all the gods. He could make anything he wanted. So great were his powers that he created people, the world and the heavens. Among other things, he was also responsible for creating the seasons, animals and plants. The powers of Ra were extraordinary and he wielded them through a hidden name in which his powers lived. Since this hidden name was known only to Ra, only he could use those powers.

8. According to a myth, goddess isis is able to steal ra's powers

While Ra had incredible power, there is a myth that suggests that he ended up becoming weak later. The story goes that Ra drooled saliva as he grew old. Isis; the goddess of marriage, fertility, magic and medicine; knew very well that Ra's powers lay hidden in his secret name. She wanted to know this secret name in order to become all-powerful herself. Isis collected Ra's saliva, mixed it with clay and made a serpent with the purpose of biting Ra. Her plan was successful. Ra was in tremendous pain after the serpent bite and he summoned other gods to help him. Isis promised to heal Ra if he let out his secret name. Since the pain was intolerable, Ra allowed Isis to search through him. Thus Ra's powers got transferred to Isis. Though she kept her promise of healing Ra, she forcibly abdicated him and made Horus the king of the gods.

9. The pharaohs ruled egypt as earthly embodiment of ra

Ra was revered as the chief-god of the pantheon of Heliopolis and the creator of everything that existed. Ancient Egyptians believed that they owed their existence to god as he created the world and Ra was the king since this day. The pharaoh, or the king, was seen as his descendant or successor. The myth goes that Ra brought order in the world of chaos and the pharaohs were meant to do the same when they came on the throne. Since 25th century BC, when Ra gained in prominence, the pharaohs often connected themselves with Ra to establish their supremacy as they wanted to be perceived as the earthly embodiment of the almighty Ra.

10. The first temple dedicated to ra was built at abusir by pharaoh userkaf

From the Fifth Dynasty or 25th century BC, Ra came to be closely associated with the pharaoh. The pharaoh of ancient Egypt since the fifth dynasty and thereafter came to be known as The Son of Ra and he even incorporated the name Ra to his name. Also, after the Fifth Dynasty, Ra became a state deity and pharaohs had specially aligned pyramids, obelisks and sun temples built in his honor. However, none of the solar temples built contained any statue of Ra. Instead, they were built with an open structure to receive sunlight, which symbolized the sun god. The first temple dedicated to Ra was built at Abusir by Pharaoh Userkaf, founder of the Fifth Dynasty.

END OF THE UNIVERSE

The ancient Egyptians believed that life on earth was only one part of an eternal journey which ended, not in death, but in everlasting joy. One was born on earth through the benevolence of the gods and the deities known as The Seven Hathors then decreed one's fate after birth; the soul then went on to live as good a life as it could in the body it had been given for a time. When death came, it was only a transition to another realm where, if one were justified by the gods, one would live eternally in a paradise known as The Field of Reeds. The Field of Reeds (sometimes called The Field of Offerings), known to the Egyptians as A'aru, was a mirror image of one's life on earth. The aim of every ancient Egyptian was to make that life worth living eternally and, as far as the records indicate, they did their very best at that.

Popular View of Egyptians as Death Obsessed
Egypt has been synonymous with tombs and mummies since the late 18th, 19th, and early 20th centuries CE when western explorers, archaeologists, entrepreneurs, showmen, and con men began investigating and exploiting the culture. The first film sensationalizing mummies, Cleopatra's Tomb, was produced in 1899 CE by George Melies. The film is now lost but, reportedly, told the story of Cleopatra's mummy which was discovered, hacked to pieces, and then revived to wreak havoc on the living. 1911 CE saw the release of The Mummy by Thanhouser Company in which the mummy of an Egyptian princess is revived through charges of electrical current and, in the end, the scientist who brings her back to life marries her. The 1922 CE discovery of the tomb of Tutankhamun was world-wide news and the story of The Curse of King Tut which followed after fascinated people as much as the photos

of the immense treasure taken from the tomb. Egypt became associated with death in the popular imagination and later films such as The Mummy (1932) capitalized on this interest. In the 1932 film, Boris Karloff plays Imhotep, an ancient priest who was buried alive, as well as the resurrected Imhotep who goes by the name of Ardath Bey. Bey is trying to murder the beautiful Helen Grosvenor (played by Zita Johann) who is the reincarnation of Imhotep's great love, Ankesenamun. In the end, Bey's plans to murder, mummify, and then resurrect Helen as her past-life incarnation of the Egyptian princess are thwarted and Bey is reduced to dust.

This film's immense box-office success guaranteed sequels which were produced throughout the 1940's (The Mummy's Hand, The Mummy's Tomb, The Mummy's Ghost, and The Mummy's Curse, 1940-1944) spoofed in the 1950's (Abbot and Costello Meet the Mummy, 1955), continued in the 1960's (The Curse of the Mummy's Tomb in `64 and The Mummy's Shroud in `67), and on to the 1971 Blood From the Mummy's Tomb. The mummy horror genre was revived with the remake of The Mummy in 1999 which was just as popular as the 1932 film, inspiring the sequel The Mummy Returns in 2001 and the films on the Scorpion King (2002-2012) which were equally well received. The recent release Gods of Egypt (2015) shifts the focus from mummies and kings to Egyptian gods and the afterlife but still promotes the association of Egypt with death and darkness through its excessively violent plot and depiction of the underworld as the abode of demons.

Mummies, curses, mystical gods and rites have been a staple of popular depictions of Egyptian culture in books as well as film for almost 200 years now all promoting the seemingly self-evident 'fact' that the ancient Egyptians were obsessed with death. This understanding is fueled by the works of early writers on ancient Egypt who misinterpreted the Egyptian's view of eternal life as obsessing over the end of one's time on earth. Even into the 20th century CE, when scholars had a better understanding of Egyptian culture, the noted historian Edith Hamilton, generally quite reliable, wrote in 1930 CE.

Egyptian View of Life
In fact, there is ample evidence that the Egyptians played a great deal. Sports which were regularly enjoyed in ancient Egypt include hockey, handball, archery, swimming, tug of war, gymnastics, rowing, and a sport known as "water jousting" which was a sea battle played in small boats on the Nile River in which a 'jouster' tried to knock the other jouster out of his boat while a second team member maneuvered the craft. Children were taught to swim at an early age and swimming was among the most popular sports which gave rise to other water games. The board game of Senet was extremely popular, representing one's journey through life to eternity. Music, dance, and carefully choreographed gymnastics were part of the major festivals and one of the chief concepts valued by the Egyptians was gratitude for the life they had been given and everything in it.
The gods were considered one's close friends and benefactors who imbued every day with meaning. Hathor was always close at hand as The Lady of the Sycamore, a tree goddess, who provided shade and comfort but was at the same time presiding over the heavenly Nile River, the Milky Way as a cosmic force and, as Lady of the Necropolis, opened the door for the departed soul to the afterlife. She was also present at every festival, wedding, and funeral as The Lady of Drunkeness who encouraged people to lighten their hearts by drinking beer.
The other gods and goddesses of Egypt are also depicted as intimately concerned with the life and welfare of human beings. During one's earthly journey they provided the living

with all of their needs and, after death, they appeared to comfort and guide the soul. Goddesses like Selket, Nephthys, and Qebhet guided and protected the newly arrived souls in the afterlife; Qebhet even brought them cool, refreshing water. Anubis, Thoth, and Osiris brought them to judgment and rewarded or punished them. The popular image of the Egyptians as death obsessed could not be more wrong; if anything, the ancient Egyptians were obsessed with life and living it abundantly.

The Egyptian afterlife was a mirror-image of life on earth. To the Egyptians, their country was the most blessed and perfect world. In ancient Greek literature one finds the famous stories of the Iliad and the Odyssey depicting great battles in a foreign land and adventures on the return journey; but no such works exist in Egyptian literature because they were not that interested in leaving their homes or their land. The Egyptian work Tale of the Shipwrecked Sailor cannot be compared with Homer's works as the characters have nothing in common and the themes are completely different. The sailor had no desire for adventure or glory, he was just going about his master's business and, unlike Odysseus, the sailor is not at all tempted by the magical island with all good things on it because he knows that the only things he wants are back home in Egypt.

"THE EGYPTIAN AFTERLIFE WAS A MIRROR-IMAGE OF LIFE ON EARTH. TO THE EGYPTIANS, THEIR COUNTRY WAS THE MOST BLESSED AND PERFECT WORLD"

Egyptian festivals encouraged living life to its fullest and appreciating the moments one had with family and friends. One's home, however modest, was deeply appreciated and so were the members of one's family and larger community. Pets were loved as dearly by the Egyptians as they are in the present day and were preserved in art works, inscriptions, and in writing, often by name. Since life in ancient Egypt was so highly valued it only makes sense that they would have imagined an afterlife which mirrored it closely.

From Life to Life
Death was only a transition, not a completion, and opened the way to the possibility of eternal happiness. When a person died, the soul was thought to be trapped in the body because it was used to this mortal home. Spells and images painted on tomb walls (known as the Coffin Texts, The Pyramid Texts, and The Egyptian Book of the Dead) and amulets attached to the body, were provided to remind the soul of its continued journey and to calm and direct it to leave the body and proceed on.

The soul would make its way toward the Hall of Truth (also known as The Hall of Two Truths) in the company of Anubis, the guide of the dead, where it would wait in line with others for judgment by Osiris. There are different versions of what would happen next but, in the most popular story, the soul would make the Negative Confessions in front of Osiris, Thoth, Anubis, and the Forty-Two Judges.

The Negative Confessions are a list of 42 sins against one's self, others, or the gods which one could honestly say one had never engaged in. Historian Margaret Bunson notes how "the Confessions were to be recited to establish the moral virtue of the deceased and his or her right to eternal bliss" (187). The Confessions would include statements such as: "I have not stolen, I have not stolen the property of a god, I have not said lies, I have not caused anyone to weep, I have not gossiped, I have not made anyone hungry" and many others. It may seem exceptionally harsh to expect a soul to go through life and never "cause anyone to weep" but it is thought that lines like this one or "I have not made anyone angry" are meant to be understood with qualification; as in "I have not caused anyone to weep unjustly" or "I have not made anyone angry without reason".

After the Negative Confessions were made, Osiris, Thoth, Anubis, and the Forty-Two Judges would confer. If one's confession was found acceptable then the soul would present its heart to Osiris to be weighed in the golden scales against the white feather of truth. If one's heart was found to be lighter than the feather, one moved on to the next phase but, if the heart was heavier, it was thrown to the floor where it was eaten by Ammut "the female devourer of the dead". This resulted in "the Great Death" which was non-existence. There was no 'hell' in the Egyptian afterlife; non-existence was a far worse fate than any kind eternal damnation.

The Field of Reeds

If the soul passed through the Weighing of the Heart it moved on to a path which led to Lily Lake (also known as the Lake of Flowers). There are, again, a number of versions of what could happen on this path where, in some, one finds dangers to be avoided and gods to help and guide while, in others, it is an easy walk down the kind of path one would have known back home. At the shore of Lily Lake the soul would meet the Divine Ferryman, Hraf-hef (He-Who-Looks-Behind-Him) who was perpetually unpleasant. The soul would have to find some way to be courteous to Hraf-hef, no matter what unkind or cruel remarks he made, and show one's self worthy of continuing the journey.

"IF THE SOUL PASSED THROUGH THE WEIGHING OF THE HEART IT MOVED ON TO A PATH WHICH LED TO LILY LAKE"

Having passed this test, the soul was brought across the waters to the Field of Reeds. Here one would find those loved ones who had passed on before, one's favorite dogs or cats, gazelles or monkeys, or whatever cherished pet one had lost. One's home would be there, right down to the lawn the way it had been left, one's favorite tree, even the stream that ran behind the house. Here one could enjoy an eternity of the life one had left behind on earth in the presence of one's favorite people, animals, and most loved possessions; and all of this in the immediate presence of the gods. Spell 110 of The Egyptian Book of the Dead is to be spoken by the deceased to claim the right to enter this paradise.

Alternate Views of the Afterlife
Bunson's note on how the view of the afterlife changed according to time and belief is reflected in some visions of the afterlife which deny its permanence and beauty. These interpretations do not belong to any one particular period but seem to crop up periodically throughout Egypt's later history. They are particularly prominent, however, in the period of the Middle Kingdom (2040-1782 BCE) expressed in texts known as The Lay of the Harper (or Songs of the Harper) and Dispute Between a Man and His Ba (soul). The Lay of the Harper is so called because the inscriptions always include an image of a harpist. They are a collection of songs which reflect on death and the meaning of life. Dispute Between a Man and his Ba comes from the collection of texts known as Wisdom Literature which are often skeptical of the afterlife.

Some of the texts which comprise The Lay of the Harper affirm life after death clearly while others question it and some deny it completely. One example from c. 2000 BCE from the stele of Intef reads, in part, "hearts at rest/Hear not the cry of mourners at the tomb/Which have no meaning to the silent dead." In Dispute Between a Man and His Ba, the man complains to his soul that life is misery but he fears death and what awaits him on the other side. In these versions, the afterlife is presented as either a myth people cling to or just as uncertain and tenuous as one's life.

In still another version, the justified dead served Ra as the crew of his solar barge as it crossed the night sky and helped defend the sun god from the serpent Apophis. In this version, the just souls are co-workers with the gods in the afterlife who help make the sun rise again for those still on earth. Their friends and relatives who were still living would greet the sunrise with gratitude for their efforts and would think of them every morning. As in all ancient cultures, remembrance of the dead was an important cultural value of the Egyptians and this version of the afterlife reflects that. Even in versions where the soul arrives in paradise it could still be called upon to man The Boat of Millions, the sun barge, to help the gods protect the light from the forces of darkness.

The Comfort of Eternity

For the greater part of Egypt's history, however, some version of the paradise of the Field of Reeds, reached after a judgment by a powerful god, prevailed. A wall painting from the tomb of the craftsman Sennedjem from the 19th Dynasty (1292-1186 BCE) depicts the soul's journey from earthly life to eternal bliss. Sennedjem is seen meeting the gods who grant him leave to pass on to paradise and is then depicted with his wife, Iyneferti, enjoying their time together in the Field of Reeds where they harvest wheat, go to work, plow their field, and harvest fruit from their trees just as they used to do on the earthly plane.

If a soul was not interested in plowing fields or harvesting grains in the afterlife, it could call on a shabti doll to do the work instead. Shabti dolls were funerary figures made of wood, stone, or faience which were placed in the tombs or graves with the dead. In the afterlife it was thought one could call on these shabtis to do one's work while one relaxed and enjoyed one's self. Spell 472 of the Coffin Texts and Spell Six of The Egyptian Book of the Dead both are instructions for the soul to call the shabti to life in the Field of Reeds.

Once the shabti went off to work, the soul could then go back to relaxing beneath a favorite tree with a good book or walk by a pleasant stream with one's dog. The Egyptian afterlife was perfect because the soul was given back everything which had been lost. One's best friend, husband, wife, mother, father, son, daughter, cherished cat or most dearly loved dog were there upon one's arrival or, at least, would be eventually; and there the souls of the dead would live forever in paradise and never have to part again. In all of the ancient world there was never a more comforting afterlife imagined by any other culture.

PART 3
CHAPTER 7

INFLUENCE IN EGYPTIAN CULTURE

Ancient Egypt, the fabled land of the pharaohs, has fascinated many historians and archaeologists. This ancient civilization has a distinctive culture with motifs familiar to most of the western world today, and still captures the imagination more readily than many other cultures of its time. This is largely due to the Egyptian style of art: colorful, consistent, monumental, and mathematical. The pyramids at Giza or the Sphinx are instantly recognized throughout the world, and these works in particular show a constant theme in Egyptian art: the reflection of the culture's metaphysical beliefs and mythology. The religious beliefs of Egyptians varied among different areas of the two kingdoms, and it would be impossible to explain every local variation of every myth here. The art of the civilization, however, seems at first to have an extremely consistent style throughout history, but upon closer inspection we see subtle nuances of evolution in Egyptian art from the Predynastic period to the New Kingdom and afterwards.
Egyptian art was influenced by several factors, including the Nile River, the two kingdoms (the Upper in the south and the Lower in the north), agriculture and hunting, animals, the heavens, the pharaohs and gods, and religious beliefs. Religion was one of the major patrons of Egyptian art throughout its three-millenium history. It was a major part of daily life, and so eventually evolved into such a complexity that it could take

books to explain each symbol and categorize each deity. Even the current king was considered a deity, and after his death he became like Osiris, the god who died and was reborn (a common mythological archetype), and lived in the underworld with the gods. Most art found in tombs featured either the pharaoh or the gods as subject, whether painting or sculpture, and made generous use of symbols to convey different layers of meaning. The symbols so apparent in Egyptian mythology could be used to either hide or reveal a message, conveyed by hieroglyphs, the ideographic written language system, or by the artwork itself, to an audience.

Sculpture is the most common example of Egyptian art that we have today, and specimens exist that date to the Predynastic period. Most of these are pottery and figurines, but these already show expressionistic qualities in the painting of the pottery, and many clay figures even represent local gods. In the Old Kingdom (roughly 2700-2100 B.C.), sculpture mainly represented the royal family members. They were portrayed in a very solid, symmetrical, blocklike fashion. The monumental Great Sphinx at Giza, constructed for Khafre (a 4th dynasty pharaoh), clearly shows this style. A portrait of the king is placed upon the body of a lion or panther, which shows his connection with the heavens, as the skies were represented earlier by a panther (Nut, the sky goddess, is shown arched over the heavens on all fours like her animal predecessor). Another deity that is shown often is Horus, the falcon god, who is seen protecting the head of Khafre in his life-size portrait. Most of these portrait statues were found in the tombs of the kings, as they were to provide a place for the king's ka, or soul, after his death.

During the Middle Kingdom (about 2000-1650 B.C.), paintings and occasional relief sculpture were found on the walls of royal tombs, which were often large rooms carved out of the sides of cliffs. Many of these depict scenes from daily life as well as those of the afterlife. The exacting details of Egyptian painting were responsible for the regularity of the subjects. Objects were drawn at their most characteristic angle, and specific canons of proportion were used for figures. For both painting and relief carving, sketches were drawn over a graph on the surface and had to be approved by a trained designer before work could begin. Small crafted objects found in tombs include faience (a glass paste used as a glaze) animal figurines and intricate jewelry made from gold and precious stones. Larger sculptures found from this era do not have the same rigidity of the Old Kingdom, but are more realistic and reflect some of the personality of the subject.

In the New Kingdom (circa 1550-1100 B.C.), many new palaces and courts were built along the Nile. Worship of the god Amun had become widespread, and it was with this deity that the pharaoh identified himself. When Amenhotep IV came to the throne in the 18th Dynasty, he managed to completely reform Egypt's religious, artistic, and political ideas by establishing what Egyptologists now believe was the first monotheistic religion- worship of Aten the solar disk as supreme being. He also changed his own name to Akhenaten ("on the behalf of Aten") and saw himself as the literal son of the sun. According to his commands, court artists' depictions of the pharaoh placed him in informal settings, often with his family. He is portrayed with distinctively odd features; this is often thought to be due to the realism he advocated in New Kingdom art. Most Egyptologists believe that the artists portrayed him with disfigurements due to royal inbreeding. However, another view suggests that his distorted form is actually a merging of female and male characteristics. The sun embodied both male and female aspects, and as representative of the sun on earth, artists portrayed Akhenaten as such.

One type of treasure from the New Kingdom that represents painting from that period is the Pert-em-Hru ("Coming Forth by Day"), also known as the Book of the Dead. This was like a guide to the underworld for the deceased, and a personal copy was included in many tombs. The Egyptian myths of the afterlife are evident in the spells and incantations that the deceased must recite to help him pass judgement: after death, the person's heart was weighed against the feather of Truth, and which way the balance fell determined whether the person was worthy to enter the underworld and live with Osiris. The heart and the feather were placed upon a balance and weighed by Thoth, who recorded the results. Those who were pure and "true of voice" were escorted by Horus into the underworld, where they lived in peace for ever. Those whose heart was heavier than the feather of Truth were destroyed by a monster known as Ammut, who was part crocodile, part lioness, and part hippopotamus. The most well-known example of these is the Scroll of Ani, painted on papyrus during the New Kingdom.

CHAPTER 8

INFLUENCE OF MYTHOLOGY IN EGYPTIAN RELIGILION

Because the Egyptians rarely described theological ideas explicitly, the implicit ideas of mythology formed much of the basis for Egyptian religious belief. The purpose of Egyptian religion was the maintenance of Ma'at, and the concepts that myths express were believed to be essential to Ma'at. The rituals of Egyptian religion were meant to make the mythic events, and the concepts they represented, real once more, thereby renewing Ma'at. The rituals were believed to achieve this effect through the force of heka, the same connection between the physical and divine realms that enabled the original creation.

For this reason, Egyptian rituals often included actions that symbolized mythological events. Temple rites included the destruction of models representing malign gods like Set or Apophis, private magical spells called upon Isis to heal the sick as she did for Horus, and funerary practices evoked the myth of Osiris' resurrection.

Yet rituals rarely, if ever, involved reenactment of entire mythic narratives. Many ritual activities were focused on more basic activities like giving offerings to the gods, with mythic themes serving as ideological background rather than as the focus of a rite. Nevertheless, myth and ritual strongly influenced each other: myths could inspire rituals, and rituals that did not originally have a mythological meaning could be reinterpreted as having one.

Kingship was a key element of Egyptian religion, through the king's role as link between humanity and the gods. Myths explain the background for this connection between royalty and divinity. The myths about the Ennead establish the king as heir to the lineage of rulers reaching back to the creator; the myth of divine birth states that the king is the son and heir of a god; and the myths about Osiris and Horus emphasize that rightful succession to the throne is essential to the maintenance of Ma'at. Thus, mythology provided the rationale for the very nature of Egyptian government.

The god-like Pharaoh of Ancient Egypt was also its chief priest, the person through whom the gods spoke. As a descendant of the first king of Egypt, (the god called Horus), he sat on the Horus throne. He protected his people by making sure that Egypt was ruled in the way the gods approved – with order, justice and stability (called maat).

Priests and priestesses wore nothing but white linens to appear clean and pure for the gods. Male priests were said to bathe as many as seven times a day and were shaved completely bald. Certain temples, mostly of Horus, would have statues that were bathed and dressed every day. Almost every Egyptian had a name involving a deity, so it would be hard to ignore such a religion. The Egyptians were so anxious about the afterlife that they spent their current-lives pleasing the gods to ensure they were accepted into the western paradise. The Pharaoh himself was seen to be a reincarnation of Horus. Whichever cult he favoured, the majority of his people would turn to. Many jewellery pieces were of "religious" base. Art was also swamped with religion. Most everything drawn or written was religious. Needless to say, the gods and goddesses were the life of the Egyptians.

Everyday Life

Religion was interwoven, not only into the pharaoh's power, but into life itself. It was the deity of a town who the people turned to, in order to prevent the everyday hazards of living. They used magic spells, charms, folklore and amulets to appealed to the deity for protection against hazards, and to negotiate on their behalf, for anything from the Nile flooding, to sowing seeds and harvesting crops, to protection from poisonous snakes, and for safe childbirth.

Egyptians spent their lives constructing their tombs, more or less excited to join their family in the afterlife with the god Osiris. Many homes and family temples have been found with usahbti figures (small mummy-form figures) and idols in a niche or space reserved in the h ome for worship. Even their writing system, cursive and heretic hieroglyphics, included figures of gods and goddesses.

Temples

There were many temples in Egypt, which indicated how essential religion was to the Ancient Egyptian people. It also indicates how essential they were to the function of everyday life and the religious function was not always the whole story. Often one temple was built so close to another that whole temple complexes, even temple cities arose, cities like Giza, or Thebes. Within these temples, the Egyptians performed a variety of rituals, the central functions of Egyptian religion; giving offerings to the gods, re-enacting their mythological interactions through festivals, and warding off the forces of chaos. These rituals were seen as necessary for the gods to continue to uphold maat, the divine order of the universe.

INFLUENCE OF MYTHOLOGY IN EGYPTIAN ART

Illustrations of gods and mythological events appear extensively alongside religious writing in tombs, temples, and funerary texts. As stated above, mythological scenes in Egyptian artwork are rarely placed in sequence as a narrative, but such scenes, particularly depicting the resurrection of Osiris, do sometimes appear individually in religious artwork. Oblique mythological allusions were very widespread in Egyptian art and architecture. In temple design, the central path of the temple axis was likened to the sun god's path across the sky, and the sanctuary at the end of the path represented the place of creation from which he rose. Temple decoration was replete with solar emblems that underscored this relationship.

Similarly, the corridors of tombs were linked with the god's journey through the Duat, and the burial chamber with the tomb of Osiris. The pyramid, the best-known of all Egyptian architectural forms, may have been inspired by mythic symbolism, for it represented the mound of creation and the original sunrise, appropriate associations for a monument intended to assure the owner's rebirth after death.

Symbols in Egyptian tradition were subject to a great deal of reinterpretation, so that the meanings of mythical symbols could change and multiply over time like the myths themselves.

More ordinary works of art were also designed to evoke mythic themes, like the amulets that Egyptians commonly wore to invoke divine powers. The Eye of Horus, for instance, was a very common shape for protective amulets because it represented Horus' well-being after the restoration of his lost eye. Scarab-shaped amulets symbolized the regeneration of life, referring to the form that Ra was said to take at dawn.

Ancient Egyptian art must be viewed from the standpoint of the ancient Egyptians to understand it. The somewhat static, usually formal, strangely abstract, and often blocky nature of much Egyptian imagery has, at times, led to unfavorable comparisons with later, and much more 'naturalistic,' Greek or Renaissance art. However, the art of the Egyptians served a vastly different purpose than that of these later cultures.

Art Not Meant To Be Seen
While today we marvel at the glittering treasures from the tomb of Tutankhamun, the sublime reliefs in New Kingdom tombs, and the serene beauty of Old Kingdom statuary, it is imperative to remember that the majority of these works were never intended to be seen—that was simply not their purpose.

The function of Egyptian art
These images, whether statues or relief, were designed to benefit a divine or deceased recipient. Statuary provided a place for the recipient to manifest and receive the benefit of ritual action. Most statues show a formal frontality, meaning they are arranged straight ahead, because they were designed to face the ritual being performed before them. Many statues were also originally placed in recessed niches or other architectural settings—contexts that would make frontality their expected and natural mode.
Statuary, whether divine, royal, or elite, provided a kind of conduit for the spirit (or ka) of that being to interact with the terrestrial realm. Divine cult statues (few of which survive) were the subject of daily rituals of clothing, anointing, and perfuming with incense and were carried in processions for special festivals so that the people could "see" them (they were almost all entirely shrouded from view, but their 'presence' was felt).

Royal and elite statuary served as intermediaries between the people and the gods. Family chapels with the statuary of a deceased forefather could serve as a sort of 'family temple.' There were festivals in honor of the dead, where the family would come and eat in the chapel, offering food for the Afterlife, flowers (symbols of rebirth), and incense (the scent of which was considered divine). Preserved letters let us know that the deceased was actively petitioned for their assistance, both in this world and the next.

What we see in museums

Generally, the works we see on display in museums were products of royal or elite workshops; these pieces fit best with our modern aesthetic and ideas of beauty. Most museum basements, however, are packed with hundreds (even thousands!) of other objects made for people of lower status— small statuary, amulets, coffins, and stelae (similar to modern tombstones) that are completely recognizable, but rarely displayed. These pieces generally show less quality in the workmanship; being oddly proportioned or poorly executed; they are less often considered 'art' in the modern sense. However, these objects served the exact same function of providing benefit to their owners (and to the same degree of effectiveness), as those made for the elite.

Modes of representation for three-dimensional art

Three-dimensional representations, while being quite formal, also aimed to reproduce the real-world statuary of gods, royalty, and the elite was designed to convey an idealized version of that individual. Some aspects of 'naturalism' were dictated by the material. Stone statuary, for example, was quite closed with arms held close to the sides, limited positions, a strong back pillar that provided support, and with the fill spaces left between limbs.

Wood and metal statuary, in contrast, was more expressive arms could be extended and hold separate objects, spaces between the limbs were opened to create a more realistic appearance, and more positions were possible. Stone, wood, and metal statuary of elite figures, however, all served the same functions and retained the same type of formalization and frontality. Only statuettes of lower status people displayed a wide range of possible actions, and these pieces were focused on the actions, which benefitted the elite owner, not the people involved.

Modes of representation for two-dimensional art

Two-dimensional art represented the world quite differently. Egyptian artists embraced the two-dimensional surface and attempted to provide the most representative aspects of each element in the scenes rather than attempting to create vistas that replicated the real world.

Each object or element in a scene was rendered from its most recognizable angle and these were then grouped together to create the whole. This is why images of people show their face, waist, and limbs in profile, but eye and shoulders frontally. These scenes are complex composite images that provide complete information about the various elements, rather than ones designed from a single viewpoint, which would not be as comprehensive in the data they conveyed.

Registers

Scenes were ordered in parallel lines, known as registers. These registers separate the scene as well as provide ground lines for the figures. Scenes without registers are unusual and were generally only used to specifically evoke chaos; battle and hunting scenes will often show the prey or foreign armies without groundlines. Registers were also used to convey information about the scenes—the higher up in the scene, the higher the status; overlapping figures imply that the ones underneath are further away, as are those elements that are higher within the register.

Hierarchy of scale
Difference in scale was the most commonly used method for conveying hierarchy—the larger the scale of the figures, the more important they were. Kings were often shown at the same scale as deities, but both are shown larger than the elite and far larger than the average Egyptian.

Text and image
Text accompanied almost all images. In statuary, identifying text will appear on the back pillar or base, and relief usually has captions or longer texts that complete and elaborate on the scenes. Hieroglyphs were often rendered as tiny works of art in themselves, even though these small pictures do not always stand for what they depict; many are instead phonetic sounds. Some, however, are logographic, meaning they stand for an object or concept.

The lines blur between text and image in many cases. For instance, the name of a figure in the text on a statue will regularly omit the determinative (an unspoken sign at the end of a word that aids identification–for example, verbs of motion are followed by a pair of walking legs, names of men end with the image of a man, names of gods with the image of a seated god, etc.) at the end of the name. In these instances, the representation itself serves this function.

INFLUENCE OF MYTHOLOGY IN EGYPTIAN LITERATURE

Themes and motifs from mythology appear frequently in Egyptian literature, even outside of religious writings. An early instruction text, the "Teaching for King Merykara" from the Middle Kingdom, contains a brief reference to a myth of some kind, possibly the Destruction of Mankind; the earliest known Egyptian short story, "Tale of the Shipwrecked Sailor", incorporates ideas about the gods and the eventual dissolution of the cosmos into a story set in the past. Some later stories derive much of their plot from mythological events: "Tale of the Two Brothers" adapts the myth of Osiris into a fantastic story about ordinary people, and "The Blinding of Truth by Falsehood" transforms the conflict between Horus and Set into an allegory.

Non-religious texts directly describing events among the gods may have appeared as early as the Middle Kingdom, and such texts are particularly abundant from the Late and Greco-Roman periods. Although these texts are more clearly derived from myth than those mentioned above, they still adapt the myths for non-religious purposes. "The Contendings of Horus and Seth" tells the story of the conflict between the two gods, often with a humorous and seemingly irreverent tone. "The Myth of the Eye of the Sun" incorporates fables into an entirely myth-based framing story.

Literary purposes could also affect the mythic narratives found in magical texts, as with "Isis, the Rich Woman's Son, and the Fisherman's Wife", which incorporates a moral message unrealated to its magical purpose. The varying attitudes and functions of these texts demonstrate the wide range of purposes that myth was adapted to serve in Egyptian culture.

CHAPTER 9

ENDING CHAPTER ABOUT HER - IMPORTANT PART OF ANCIENT EGYPT

Ancient Egyptian Gods
Ancient Egyptian gods were an important part of ancient Egyptian religion. This belief was so strong in ancient Egypt that throughout the nation's history various pharaohs would stop at nothing to insure the public believed they had received the divine right to rule from the gods themselves. They tried to understand their place in the universe and their mythology centers itself on nature, the earth, sky, moon, sun, stars, and the Nile River. This is where the cosmic creation of Egyptian myth began. Ancient Egyptian mythology states that in the beginning of time everything began with Nu.
Unlike other ancient cultures, whose gods looked somewhat like people, Egyptian gods had animal heads. Ra was the most important of the gods. The worship of Ra really began when the Egyptians began building pyramids to and for Ra. They believed that Ra was the creator of the world and of life. Ra, the god of light, was often referred to as the Great Cat. In Ancient Egypt, family members shaved their eyebrows in mourning when the family cat died. In those days killing a cat was a crime punishable by death. The cat was considered sacred and worshiped by mumitizing them before burial. In one ancient city in Egypt, more than 300,000 cat mummies were found.
Anubis is frequently the deity referred to as the god of death. Like many other ancient Egyptian gods Anubis is most

frequently associated with the jackal, an animal that is representative of tombs and death. Despite all the other ancient gods Anubis received the most cult worship in the city of Cynopolis. In a mythological tradition that encompasses innumerable Egyptian gods, Anubis is seen as the guide who directs the dead either to Osiris or the worse fate of Ammit. Rather than any of the other ancient Egyptian gods Anubis was chosen to take a prominent place in the tomb of King Tutankhamun. Annubis is also sometimes known as Anpu and Inepu and is believed to have been married to Anput; according to popular Egyptian mythology. It is believed that of all the ancient Egyptian gods Anubis is perhaps one of the oldest. Many tales suggest that Anubis might even out date Osiris; one of the most prominent of the Egyptian deities.

During the three thousand year history of the polytheistic religion of Egypt was comprised of a very complex system of Egyptian gods and goddesses. Even the Egyptian recognized the difficulty of following the multitude of gods and goddesses as early as the Old Kingdom. The Egyptian gods can be divided into two main categories; household gods and local, state or national gods.

Horus the Egyptian falcon god is known by many names throughout Egypt, however he is most commonly associated with the falcon. Seth the Egyptian god is also referred to as Setekh and Set. He was often believed to be in conflict with Horus Egyptian falcon god. At various times throughout the history of Egypt, the two deities competed for popularity and power among the Egyptian people. One of the most famous legends involving Isis putting the body of her husband back together after he was killed by Seth the Egyptian god, impregnating herself with his body and giving birth to their son Horus Egyptian falcon god. Ancient Egyptian crocodile gods are quite prominent within Egyptian mythology. Sobek, is another well known god associated with the crocodile. He is usually seen either completely as a crocodile or as a combination between human form and crocodile, symbolizing the strength of the Egyptian pharaohs.

CHAPTER 10

CONCLUSION

Egyptian mythology is the collection of myths from ancient Egypt, which describe the actions of the Egyptian gods as a means of understanding the cosmos. Myth appears frequently in Egyptian writings and art, particularly in short stories and in religious material such as hymns, ritual texts, funerary texts, and temple decoration. These sources rarely contain a complete account of a myth and often describe only brief fragments. This lack of narrative in myth-related writings has prompted debate among scholars about whether cohesive myths existed in ancient Egyptian culture.

Inspired by the cycles of nature, the Egyptians saw time in the present as a series of recurring patterns, whereas the earliest periods of time were linear. Myths are set in these earliest times, and myth sets the pattern for the cycles of the present. Present events repeat the events of myth, and in doing so renew Ma'at, the fundamental order of the cosmos.

Amongst the most important episodes from the mythic past are the creation myths, in which the gods form the universe out of primordial chaos; the stories of the reign of the sun god Ra upon the earth; and the myth of Osiris and Isis, concerning the struggles of the gods Osiris, Isis, and Horus against the disruptive god Set. Events from the present that might be regarded as myths include Ra's daily journey through the world and its otherworldly counterpart, the Duat. Recurring themes in these mythic episodes include the conflict between the upholders of Ma'at and the forces of disorder, the importance of the pharaoh in maintaining Ma'at, and the continual death and regeneration of the gods.

The details of these sacred events differ greatly from one text to another and often seem contradictory. All Egyptian myths, however, are meant primarily as symbols, expressing the behavior and essence of the mysterious deities in metaphorical terms. Each variant of a myth represents a somewhat different symbolic perspective, enriching the Egyptians' understanding of the gods and the world.

Mythology profoundly influenced Egyptian culture. It formed much of the basis for ancient Egyptian religion, inspiring or influencing many of its rituals and providing the ideological basis for kingship. Scenes and symbols from myth appeared in art in tombs, temples, and amulets. In literature, myths or elements of them were used in stories that range from humor to allegory, demonstrating mythology's prevalence and versatility in Egyptian tradition.

There is some debate among Egyptologists about which of the beliefs in ancient Egypt should be classed as myth. The basic definition of myth suggested by John Baines is "a sacred or culturally central narrative". In Egypt, the narratives central to culture and religion are almost entirely about events among the gods.

Actual narratives about the gods' actions are rare in Egyptian texts, particularly from early periods, and most references to such events are mere mentions or allusions. Some Egyptologists, like Baines, contend that narratives complete enough to be called "myths" existed in all periods, but that Egyptian tradition did not favor writing them down. Others, like Jan Assmann, have argued that true myths were rare in Egypt and may only have emerged partway through its history. Recently, however, scholars like Vincent Arieh Tobin and Susanne Bickel have suggested that lengthy narration is unnecessary, and even alien to, the complex and flexible nature of Egyptian mythology, because narratives tend toward a simple and fixed perspective on the events they describe. If the requirement for narration is discarded, any statement that conveys an idea about the workings of the cosmos by describing the nature or actions of a god can be called "mythic".

DISCLAIMER

All the material contained in this book is provided for educational and informational purposes only. No responsibility can be taken for any results or outcomes resulting from the use of this material. While every attempt has been made to provide information that is both accurate and effective, the author does not assume any responsibility for the accuracy or use/misuse of this information.

Made in the USA
Monee, IL
23 April 2022

95297295R00059